Praise for *We're*

"Master teacher David Michael Slate... is written in clear and concise prose that has the impa... m-mer as the author dismantles one myth after another and makes common-sense solutions to seemingly intractable problems. *We're Doing It Wrong* is a cogent and concise appraisal of the dismal state of American public education that should become mandatory reading for every concerned parent, administrator, school board member, elected public official, journalist, and self-appointed 'expert' who professes to know the easy solution to the failures of our schools. His blunt, no-holds barred assessment of the growing crisis in public schools cannot be easily dismissed. Unfortunately, the fact that he is an experienced and successful teacher will probably disqualify him in the eyes of most educational reformers who have never taught a single minute in our beleaguered schools. This is the most important, commonsense approach to fixing our public schools that I have ever been privileged to read."

—Richard O. Davies
Distinguished Professor of History, Emeritus
Academic Vice President of University of Nevada
Nevada Professor and Researcher of the Year
Dean of College of Public Service at Northern Arizona
Former President of University of Northern Colorado
Nevada Writer Hall of Fame inductee

"It is perhaps no surprise that in an age of ideologically polarized educational research and politics—matched with a widespread disrespect for teachers and public schools—a book of such straightforward sanity as this one needs to be published and read widely. It will miff people at the poles of opinion, but it is thoroughly supported by empirical research and experienced teachers' craft knowledge."

—James Paul Gee
Regents' Professor, Arizona State University
Mary Lou Fulton Presidential Professor of Literacy Studies
Member, National Academy of Education

"If you want a book with fresh ideas on perennial issues in education that are commonly and deeply misunderstood, David Michael Slater's *We're Doing It Wrong* is a relentless page-turner. Everything old is reinterpreted with new understandings and an invitation to act differently: school choice, merit pay and accountability, scripted curriculum, high-needs parents, sage or guide, tenure, and nineteen other ideas are sliced and diced in new ways. This is a 'makes you think' treatment of major myths and education conundrums—read it, and think and act differently."

—Michael Fullan
Professor Emeritus, University of Toronto

"From the moment I started reading David Michael Slater's *We're Doing It Wrong: 25 Ideas in Education That Just Don't Work—And How to Fix Them*, I thought, 'WOW . . . this guy really gets it!' It would benefit every teacher, administrator, school board member, parent, and legislator to read this book."

—Shelly Vroegh
2017 Iowa Teacher of the Year

"With a passionate voice, David Michael Slater identifies the challenges we face in education and addresses them one by one. His words encourage the visionary administrators and courageous teachers who meet these challenges head-on, and they provide a starting point for others to activate conversations that move education forward."

—Jayne Ellspermann
President, National Association of Secondary School Principals
2015 National Principal of the Year

"I finally found a book that I can relate to, ascribe to, and wholeheartedly hand to a colleague without reservations. It is rare that you find a book that contains a 'no nonsense' approach to the problems that are prevalent in our profession and solutions that offer a light at the end of the tunnel. A must-read for educators in our turbulent educational climate!"

—Brita Scott
La Grande Education Association President
Eastern Oregon UniServ Council President

"I am inspired by David's empathetic and unapologetic acknowledgement that our choice of educational transformation must honor human interaction and encourage passion."

—Joe D. Genasci, NCC NCSC
President and CEO GuidEd Fusion Inc.

"Every school board member in the country should read this book and start a community discussion about where education goes from here and how we move from a system that fails too many to one that truly serves the needs of children, educators, and the world."

—Leigh Anne Jasheway, BA, MPH
Instructor at University of Oregon School of Journalism and Communications
Recipient of the Erma Bombeck Award for Humor Writing

"I encourage not only educators and leaders to read this book, but also all policymakers and anyone else concerned or connected to our educational system. We need to remember that complex solutions are not always better. Simple is just as elegant—especially when they work."

—Robert O. Davies, PhD
President, Murray State University

"You'll find this book a provocative antidote to the educational 'deform' movement and its well-heeled advocates."

—Gregory Smith
Emeritus Professor, Graduate School of Education
and Counseling, Lewis & Clark College

"The book is deeply honest, compelling, and real and should be read by every education policymaker, leader, teacher, and community member. Thank you, David, for this provocative call to action."

—Dyan Smiley
Education advocate

"David Michael Slater's book should be required reading for the new President and Congress. His is a straight-shooting voice with thoughtful and sobering reflections directly from the field. We need to heed the compelling insights and solutions laid out in his new book about our system of education."

—Cindy Cisneros
VP of Education Programs, Committee for Economic Development

"David Michael Slater puts the conventional wisdom on education under a microscope and finds much of it wanting. I found insights on every page of this concise, engaging book."

—Jonathan Plucker, PhD
Author of *Intelligence 101*
Julian C. Stanley Professor of Talent Development at Johns Hopkins University

"David Michael Slater provides an inspiring, useful blend of 30,000-foot flyovers and boots-on-the-ground practical ideas. Any stakeholder in education—teachers, parents, and especially policymakers—will benefit from his vision and suggestions."

—Matt Miller
Teacher, speaker, and author of *Ditch That Textbook*

"Slater's book is a step in the right direction towards improving education of the next generations."

—Pam Ertel
2017 Nevada Teacher of the Year

"David Michael Slater does quite an impressive job of writing in a perspective that all teachers can relate to. As an educator, I am grateful to see these vital concerns addressed by a classroom teacher. If we want to see changes in education, we have to speak up. Slater shows no hesitation in letting his voice be heard. This is a must-read for any educator that is looking for change."

—Joni Smith
2017 Louisiana Teacher of the Year

"It is rare to find such a passionate, articulate, honest, insightful book about our educational system. I hope that this book will be read by those just beginning their careers as teachers and administrators as well as those with years of experience. It deserves as far-reaching an audience as possible."

—Robert Brooks, PhD
Psychologist and faculty (part-time), Harvard Medical School
Co-author: *Raising Resilient Children* and *Understanding and Managing Children's Classroom Behavior*

We're Doing It Wrong

25 Ideas in Education That Just Don't Work— And How to Fix Them

David Michael Slater

Skyhorse Publishing

Skyhorse Publishing books may be purchased in bulk at special discounts for sales promotion, corporate gifts, fund-raising, or educational purposes. Special editions can also be created to specifications. For details, contact the Special Sales Department, Skyhorse Publishing, 307 West 36th Street, 11th Floor, New York, NY 10018 or info@skyhorsepublishing.com.

Skyhorse® and Skyhorse Publishing® are registered trademarks of Skyhorse Publishing, Inc.®, a Delaware corporation.

Visit our website at www.skyhorsepublishing.com.

10 9 8 7 6 5 4 3 2 1

Library of Congress Cataloging-in-Publication Data is available on file.

Cover design by Jane Sheppard
Cover photography by iStockphoto

Print ISBN: 978-1-5107-2561-4
eBook ISBN: 978-1-5107-2562-1

Printed in the United States of America

For Mom—Wish you were here

Contents

Acknowledgments

Few tasks are more daunting for authors of fiction than drumming up advanced reviews. So I was not particularly optimistic when the editor of this, my first work of nonfiction, asked me to approach experts for endorsements. (Thank you, Chamois Holschuh, for seeing the potential in this manuscript.) Dutifully, I began reaching out anyway.

The response amazed me.

Dozens of accomplished and surely overburdened educators were willing to read a draft of this book. I was humbled and honored by this and in no small way inspired by the generosity of those whose calling it is to teach.

I want to thank everyone who found *We're Doing It Wrong* worthy of their endorsement—their names accompany their thoughts, so I won't re-list them here. I offer my sincerest appreciation to you all. Thank you, Jenny Hoy, for getting the ball rolling with your generous contacts.

But I'd also like recognize those who went even farther beyond the call of duty by offering detailed feedback on early drafts, whether or not they ultimately gave it their stamp of approval. You all improved this book dramatically: Kwesi Rollins, Dr. Frank Lyman, Dr. Jonathan Plucker, Tracy Horodyski, Sydney Chaffee, Dr. Eric Jensen, Dr. Connie Hebert, Dr. Barbara Blackburn, Jacie Bejster, Amy Junge, Kate Walsh, Pamela Ertel, Charlotte Danielson, Faith Boninger, John Watson, and my friend and colleague, Joe Pazar. Thank you, Sascha Perrins, for your advice (in all things). I am also grateful for the help of my longtime pal and tireless advocate for equity in education, Patricia Julianelle.

Education is, if nothing else, a never-ending conversation. So I must also thank you, kind reader, for allowing me to participate in yours.

—DMS

Foreword
This Book Will Be Misunderstood

Everyone blames teachers—it's one of our favorite national pastimes. Students blame them. Parents blame them. Administrators blame them. Politicians blame them. Teachers are incompetent. They are unfair. They are uncaring. Their standards are too low. Their standards are too high. They are sexist. They are racist. They are overpaid, lazy, predatory, agenda-driven brainwashers in it for the excessive vacation time and health-care benefits.

No profession is more unfairly maligned.[1]

And what have we here? Yet another teacher-bashing screed about how educators are *doing it wrong?*

No.

This book is *not* meant to bash teachers. I'm a writer, but I'm also a full-time teacher. I know firsthand that the vast majority of us do our very best every single day. We put in untold, unpaid hours under sometimes appalling circumstances—often not only thanklessly but in the face of bogus and insulting charges like those listed above. But that does not mean our profession isn't riddled with bad ideas that make an already difficult job even harder. These bad ideas come from parents, policymakers, administrators, and, yes, even teachers—but also from the very nature of our ill-conceived education system itself.

Regardless, these problems must be faced head-on if faith in our most precious institution is ever to be restored. In this book, I attempt to do my small part to help make that happen.

Note

1   The reason why teachers are so disrespected in America lies beyond the scope of this book. There are many explanations, of course, but there are at least two that aren't given enough consideration: 1) teaching is a mostly female profession in a sexist society; and 2) teachers do not produce measurable wealth in a materialistic society.

Disclaimer

I taught 7th grade English for thirteen years in a large Oregon school district. My students were predominantly of low socioeconomic status. I then moved to an "option" public high school that actively recruited students not succeeding in the comprehensive programs. I taught dual-credit college-writing courses there for three years, and during that time I was honored as the City of Beaverton's Educator of the Year. I now teach English to 7th and 8th graders in a Gifted and Talented program in a large Nevada public school system. I have a BA in Organizational Psychology, a Master's in Teaching, and another in English. So while my experience may not be the world's broadest, I've been around long enough now to see all manner of education "reform" ideas come and go . . . and come back again—often repackaged with new names.

In this book, I argue that there are four primary reasons bad ideas find their way into our classrooms and then present 25 prime examples, followed by solutions. But this is not a doctoral thesis. While some research is cited, my arguments are based primarily on observations made during my many years in the classroom. This is only partly because I am not a researcher. Mostly it's because, while I respect research (especially surveys of research) and believe it deserves a seat at the table, I challenge the idea that it is the *only* seat at the table. After all, it's not difficult to find equally important studies with opposite findings. So when research or reform ideas (which often have no basis in research) contradict the common sense and experience of educators who actually teach, it's not the educators that must be questioned.

My goal here is to bring common sense and experience to the table.

The critiques and suggestions in this book are meant to spur further investigation should you find them compelling enough, and I am confident that you will. For example, the one about merit pay, an idea which seems reasonable in theory but in practice would backfire spectacularly. And the one about class size—how it doesn't matter that some studies show it doesn't matter . . . since they ignore what they can't measure.

I don't count myself among the legions of alarmists who claim our public schools are raging grease fires, especially given the monumental task they are expected to accomplish. However, I'm pretty sure that, regardless of your political persuasion, you already agree that they can be drastically improved—that they *must* be drastically improved. It's my best hope that this little book might help us find some critical places where we can begin that process.

Introduction

Idea #1

Perhaps the most obvious and disturbing reason that ideas in education turn out to be duds (or much worse) is that they are so often conceived by people *who have no training in education.* Is there any other profession so powerfully influenced by people with no background in it? Is there any other field of endeavor that pretty much *everyone* thinks they are qualified to weigh in on authoritatively? Consult the résumés of your local school board—it's very likely that not a single member has a degree, let alone any practical experience, in education. It defies reason that actual educators are so seldom represented when education policies are set.

> **Idea #1:** When people with no training in education set education policy, bad ideas will find their way into classrooms.

Idea #2

Politics contribute to bad ideas reaching our classrooms in another way. Because the truth is often politically inexpedient, lawmakers frequently set education policy that flies in the face of reality. And thus educators find themselves forced to pretend things are true that simply aren't. (And there we may already have the explanation for why teachers are so rarely involved in education policy-making.)

For example, teachers these days must affirm that *all* students in their classrooms can be educated to the highest standards (say to college readiness) no matter what challenges their students face.

Which is just not true.

Admitting this does not equal giving up on anyone. No one requires doctors to declare themselves capable of bringing everyone in their care up to a minimum (high) standard of health—that they will "leave no patient behind." Rather, medical professionals take an oath to try their best and to do no harm. And no one accuses them of not caring about the sickest people they treat, *even if they literally die.* Acknowledging the limitations of public schools would change nothing but our orientation to reality.

Similarly, educators must pretend they are capable of providing equally effective service to sometimes forty or more students in a single class—forget who's hungry, abused, homeless, or taking drugs—with skill levels ranging from nearly illiterate to several years beyond grade level.

Which just can't be done.

But guess what—politicians know all of this perfectly well.

So why do they regularly set standards they know cannot and will not be met? Because they may not be reelected if they appear not to believe everyone can reach the top. Because in America we believe everyone can reach the top, no matter what. In fact, it's *un-American* to suggest otherwise. We need only to hold the right people accountable to make it happen.

The inevitable result? Failure. And more blame for teachers. After which the standards are changed (or more likely renamed), and we do the dance all over again.

The only constant is blaming teachers.

Idea #1 + #2: When people with no training in education set education policy and politics force teachers to ignore reality, bad ideas will find their way into classrooms.

Idea #3

Teaching is a science. In fact, all good teachers are scientists. They assess educational needs, experiment with pedagogy, test the results, and then adjust accordingly. But far more than it is a science, teaching is an art. Our blindness to this truth is the third reason so many bad ideas trickle down into our classrooms.

The ramifications of viewing teaching strictly as a science cannot be overstated. First, it's partly responsible for our general cultural disrespect of teachers, who are essentially viewed as replaceable factory workers who need only to follow precise instructions to produce the desired results. Second, because we think teaching is primarily a science, we foolishly imagine that when an idea is proven effective in one circumstance, it must therefore work . . . *everywhere*. Third, this notion is the reason we are standardized testing our students to death. And finally, because we have no regard for the art of teaching, brilliant, creative, artistic teachers are leaving the profession in droves.

Idea #1 + #2 + #3: When people with no training in education set education policy, when politics force teachers to ignore reality, and when teaching is viewed as more of a science than an art, bad ideas will find their way into classrooms.

Idea #4

One more thought before we dive in: sometimes perfectly good ideas make their way toward classrooms—only to go bad when they get there. This happens for a couple of reasons. Most great education ideas are complex, despite the catchy, oversimplified packaging they usually get (recently: growth mindset). Teachers often don't have enough time to learn more than a superficial version of these ideas, and so they implement them poorly. Or, just as likely, they are instructed by their administration to add this new and actually great idea to their already overfilled plates, and the best they can do is a cursory version that does little justice to or, worse, defeats its very purpose.

Idea #1 + #2 + #3 + #4: When people with no training in education set education policy, when politics force teachers to ignore reality, and when teaching is viewed as more of a science than an art, bad ideas will find their way into classrooms. Good ideas that reach classrooms will go bad if teachers aren't given time to implement them properly.

Old School
Age-Based Education

!

Problem

There's a flaw so fundamentally embedded in the system that it virtually *is* the system: age-grouping. And it cannot be defended on pedagogical grounds. We do it simply because it's far easier to organize and budget a factory-model operation than one in constant flux. Be that as it may, the age-based model is the source of many of our most persistent problems when it comes to delivering quality instruction.

First, there is the issue of social promotion, which is the practice of promoting students to the next grade regardless of whether they pass their classes—or, more to the point, learn anything. This presents a catch-22 because, perhaps unsurprisingly, students held back with younger peers often feel shamed and thus tend to fail again (also because they often receive no other interventions). But passing a pupil who failed up the ladder seems almost criminal. In fact, according to researchers, "Neither grade retention nor social promotion is an effective remedy for addressing the needs of students who are experiencing academic, behavioral, or social and emotional difficulties."[1]

It's a time-honored but lamentable tradition for teachers to blame colleagues in the lower grades for sending them students without the prerequisite skills for learning in their class. Then, after failing to fix the problem, they send the same students on to the teachers in the next grade up, who will then, in turn, blame them. I did this just about every year I taught regular ed 7th grade because I had neither the training nor the time, for example, to teach a middle schooler how to read beyond 3rd-grade level—or the power to make a student who refused to work in the face of all interventions . . . *work*.

If students were never grouped by age to begin with, there would be far less of a stigma were it decided that retention is needed. And if they could take whatever class they were ready for, it wouldn't be grade retention at all. It would be course retention, which wouldn't be remotely as damaging to a student's social standing.

How about the absurd range of skills teachers are forced to pretend they can address through "Differentiation"?[2] I often had classes of thirty-five students: five or six identified as SPED (special education) for entirely different reasons; another five or six not in SPED, but who were nonetheless years behind in their skills; three or four gifted learners; four ELLs (English-language learners); two or three with severe behavior issues; and so on. If you think that sounds like an exaggeration, please visit any random public middle school classroom. Courses not grouped by age would still have some spread of skill levels, but you'd never see students who can barely read sitting in the same room with peers who can understand college-level material.

How about the very valid complaint that teachers essentially teach to the "average" student (or neglect the highfliers because "accountability" measures force them to focus almost exclusively on low achievers)? It's extremely common, and my experience bears this out, that when schools set improvement goals for a given year, they tend to focus on moving students whose scores fall just below whatever cutoff the state punishes them for failing to reach to just above that score. This is logical behavior, of course, because moving those "bubble" students over the line (which often doesn't require dramatic improvement) has, by far, the most impact on a school's rating.

If students were grouped by readiness rather than age, "bubble" students would be with other bubble students and their teachers could focus on exactly what they need. And the same could be said about all the other students at whatever levels they operate.

And imagine the radically different social atmosphere in schools where it's entirely normal to know and spend time with people outside of one's age-group.

Solution

As recently reported in *Duke Today*, researchers at the Duke University Talent Identification Program and Northwestern University conducted an exhaustive review of educational research. They found that "after looking carefully at 100 years of research, it became clear that acceleration and most forms of ability grouping can be powerfully effective interventions . . . They help increase academic achievement for both lower- and higher-achieving students."[3]

Critics claim that ability or readiness grouping is "tracking," and evidence from the past shows, indeed, an untenable number of students, once placed on their "track," never left it. And because many of those on lower tracks were poor and/or minorities, tracking was deemed a tool of oppression and/or structural racism. (In 2014, the Department of Education found, for example, that a New Jersey school district's tracking policies were denying black students equal access to advanced- and higher-learning opportunities.)[4] But tools can be used for good or ill. Readiness groups must be fluid and flexible, and students should move up to more challenging levels when they demonstrate . . . readiness. If that is not happening, *we're doing it wrong.*

Critics also claim that students placed in lower-level classes have their self-esteem irreparably damaged. Though, I've never understood how putting students into classes for which they are not prepared—or worse, misleading them about what skills they do or do not have—could promote self-esteem (at least the healthy kind that benefits one in life).

My dream system works something like old-school swim lessons. Back in the day, when I was forced to take them, my instructor stood by with a list of strokes and checked off each one when I mastered it. When the list was done, I earned the badge and moved on to the next level. That's how I'd run schools.

In lower grades, students would need to earn skill-based badges, enough of which, in certain combinations, would earn them Levels (like passing an age grade). In secondary school, there might be college-approved course badges, like Biology or British Literature. And courses should be broken down into nine-week blocks so they can frequently be offered and repeated much more easily if failed. (Perhaps high-distinction badges could be awarded to those who earn them with superior performance.)

But here is a key element of my dream, non-age-grouped Badge system: children would be allowed to leave school at the age of sixteen.

Three groups would take advantage of this option.

The first would be students who have completed the requirements for their diploma early. There is no good reason for preventing students from graduating ahead of schedule if they can do so. (This also means, of course, allowing them to take advanced classes whenever they are ready for them.)

The second group would be students certain that college is not in their plans and who wish to enter the workforce as soon as possible. They could earn badges by sixteen which certify them for certain vocational work. More advanced vocational badges might take more years to earn.

The third group would simply be dropouts. Why is this okay? *Because students not ready to learn don't learn.*

But here's the kicker regarding the latter two groups: there would be no age limit for access to public education. If they aren't ready for Level 10 (for whatever reason) until they are twenty-nine, thirty-nine, or even seventy-nine, they are welcome back.[5]

I believe this is a compassionate system. It gives students what they need when they need it, recognizes that there is no shame in vocational careers, and, perhaps most importantly, it acknowledges that public schools cannot solve all of society's problems, chiefly poverty and the many issues associated with it. This system recognizes that the challenges in some children's lives make it impossible for them to be learners during the time they are given for that task.

By no stretch is it implied that all means would not be exhausted to keep students in school—but what's new is that if those means are exhausted, the system would finally be equipped to say, "Okay, we did our best. Come back when you're ready. We'll be here for you."

Notes

1 Shane R. Jimmerson and Tyler L Renshaw, "Retention and Social Promotion," *Principal Leadership* (September 12, 2012): 12–16, Downloads/NASSP_Grade_Retention_Sept_2012.pdf.
2 More on Differentiation in chapter 10, "Extreme Teaching."
3 Katy Munger, "New Analysis Finds Two Measures Boost K–12 Academic Achievement," *Duke Today,* December 6, 2016, accessed February 7, 2017, https://today.duke.edu/2016/12/new-analysis-finds -two-measures-boost-k-12-academic-achievement.
4 U.S. Department of Education, "U.S. Department of Education Announces Resolution of South Orange-Maplewood, N.J., School District Civil Rights Investigation," U.S. Department of

Education, October 28, 2014, www.ed.gov/news/press-releases
/us-department-education-announces-resolution-south-orange
-maplewood-nj-school-di.

5 No, we could not have twenty-nine-year-olds sitting in classrooms
with eleven-year-olds. We would need to open adult versions of public
schools in every city for students over the age of eighteen.

2

Sameness

Goals vs. Methods

❗ Problem

There is a teacher shortage, and it is only getting worse.[1] Eventually, we will have a full-blown crisis on our hands. It might not be until we reach such a point that we face the fact that teaching is becoming an ever-increasingly undesirable job—and the many reasons this is so. Educators have historically been willing to put up with a lot: disrespect, unpaid hours, out-of-pocket expenses, blame for poor student choices—but what's becoming intolerable is the steady de-professionalization of their jobs.

We know that "lack of discretion" over how they perform their duties contributes powerfully to a teacher's job dissatisfaction—and that job dissatisfaction is the number one reason educators quit.[2] And yet, over the past decade, teachers report feeling less and less autonomous in their classrooms.[3]

They are feeling like robots.

The trend to de-professionalize teachers is greatly influenced by our current obsession with conformity. We must all embrace the latest "best practice." Whether it's a curricular model, a teaching style, a school climate initiative, or a test we must teach to—if there's evidence it worked somewhere, it must work *everywhere*. And we must all use the same materials too: the same units, the same novels, etc. Otherwise, how can we compare everyone to everyone else . . . everywhere? A study published in *The American Education Research Journal* analyzed the ways schools seek to spur "reform." It found that "such influence occurs in similar ways: by centralizing and restricting the flow of information; by constricting control; by emphasizing routinized and simplified instructional/assessment practices; and by applying strong pressure for school personnel to conform."[4]

Sameness in education is foolish on many levels.

First of all, teachers with enough experience witness a very enlightening phenomenon: they see colleagues with not only different but polar opposite teaching styles both achieving successful results. Perhaps one teacher runs a "Student-Centered" classroom that stresses cooperative learning, while the other is more "old-school," delivering (highly engaging) lecture-heavy lessons. Importantly, neither could pull off what the other does.

Here's what I know: a great teacher can make the curriculum or teaching model you despise work beautifully, and a lousy one will bore students to tears with the one you extol. These days, educators who do not toe the latest line, regardless of how well they instill a love of learning in their students, are being made to feel worthless by their bosses.

The consequence of this alarming trend was addressed by renowned educator Rafe Esquith in the *Wall Street Journal,* wherein he notes that we are becoming dependent on the teachers who "quietly rebel against the current trends of standardization and uniformity."[5] How long will such rebels remain among us? Enforcing uniformity is a prescription for driving out good teachers and discouraging new ones from entering the field.

Second, our obsession with exalting methods over goals is evidence that teachers simply aren't trusted to do their jobs anymore.

Why in the world would anyone care how Mr. Rosen goes about teaching probability if his students hit their learning targets? If Mr. Stern is mad about his unit on *Hamlet* and meets the English department's objectives teaching it, what would it matter if none of his colleagues teach that play? Yet teachers are often pressured to give up their "sacred cows" (favorite units) to be team players.

A colleague shared her father-in-law's depressing story. He is a social studies teacher beloved for his passionate portrayals of historical characters (in full regalia with elaborate props). After twenty years of successfully motivating students this way, he was told by his principal that he was expected to be doing the same thing as all the other social studies teachers in the school, in fact, the same thing on the same days. Because none of this unique educator's colleagues felt capable of emulating his theatricality, he was forced to shelf the reenactments in favor of video clips and PowerPoints. He is now counting the days until retirement.

I want every educator teaching every one of their sacred cows. Don't you?

It is acknowledged that allowing diversity of approach can cause less-than-ideal situations when students change schools or even classrooms. For example, a student may find herself having to re-read a book her previous teacher already taught. But so what? What a small price to pay to have her in a classroom taught by two teachers using materials that motivate them to inspire their students.

One more point here: those of us who've been around long enough (we're the crotchety old grumps rolling our eyes in the back of the staff meeting) know that this supposedly newfangled magic bullet of an idea will eventually go away, anyway. I recently learned that new teachers in one district are being told that the days when all students in a class read the same novel "are over" because "best practice" now indicates that doing "close reads" (critical analyses focusing on details of shorter material) yields better results. But, trust me, someone will soon figure out what's lost in banishing the class novel, and they'll be back. ("Best practice," by the way, is a term that now primarily refers to teaching strategies alleged to increase student achievement on standardized assessments.)

We grumps know the pendulum is always swinging back and forth and that anyone who claims there is *any* single solution that solves any serious problem in education is either naive or selling something (or both).

Solution

I would never advocate for an "anything goes" approach to education or suggest that all teaching styles and curricular models are created equal. There are clearly unacceptable practices (like, say, using humiliation as a motivator). But I would start with the simple recognition that many roads lead to Rome. The primary focus and agreement should be on goals, not methods (goals that do not amount to passing high-stakes corporate tests). Once those are established, educators must be allowed the freedom to select from the wide array of effective practices and to choose materials they are passionate about.[6] While it is true that both the best and worst teachers seek maximum autonomy, it is incumbent upon their supervisors to know the difference between them.

So when is it reasonable to criticize a teacher for their pedagogical choices and mandate others be made? Only when they demonstrably aren't working.

Notes

1   Joe Heim, "America Has a Teacher Shortage, and a New Study Says It's Getting Worse," *Washington Post*, September 14, 2016, www

.washingtonpost.com/local/education/america-has-a-teacher-short age-and-a-new-study-says-its-getting-worse/2016/09/14/d5de1cee -79e8-11e6-beac-57a4a412e93a_story.html.

2   Tim Walker, "Want to Reduce the Teacher Shortage? Treat Teach-ers like Professionals," *NEA Today*, October 13, 2015, neatoday.org /2015/08/26/want-to-reduce-the-teacher-shortage-treat-teachers-like -professionls/.

3   Dinah Sparks and Nat Malkus, "Public School Teacher Autonomy in the Classroom across School Years 2003–04, 2007–08, and 2011– 12," *Statistics in Brief: Public School Teacher Autonomy in the Classroom across School Years 2003–04, 2007–08, and 2011–12* no. 089 (De-cember 2015): 8, http://nces.ed.gov/pubs2015/2015089.pdf.

4   Brad Olsen and Dena Sexton, "Threat Rigidity, School Reform, and How Teachers View Their Work Inside Current Education Policy Contexts," *American Educational Research Journal* 46, no. 1 (March 1, 2009): 9–44, doi:10.3102/0002831208320573.

5   Rafe Esquith, "Why Great Teachers Are Fleeing the Profession," *Washington Post*, July 17, 2013, blogs.wsj.com/speakeasy/2013/07/17 /why-great-teachers-are-fleeing-the-profession/.

6   A department will naturally choose to purchase materials to pur-sue agreed-upon goals—for example, a set of novels. They certainly couldn't be expected to buy a different set for a teacher with his own "sacred cow." But he should be free to purchase it himself if he is so inclined.

3

Can It
Scripted Curricula

Problem

The logical extension of this sameness approach and the ultimate expression of de-professionalization in education is the "canned curriculum." This is an increasingly common practice that requires educators to teach from a purchased curriculum, one containing lessons preplanned for every single day. But they are frequently less lesson plans than scripts. And teachers are often expected to read them word-for-word without deviation, regardless in some cases of how they are received by students. A 4th-grade teacher I know was required to have her class chant letter sounds and sight words with "fidelity" to a script, despite the presence of gifted and high-achieving students in the group. ("Fidelity" has become a weaponized word used to enforce conformity.) A would-be teacher interviewing for a job at a Rochester charter school was asked to read a four-page lesson plan word-for-word to demonstrate his fitness for the job. He was told that the school "has perfectly good lessons, so why waste time planning?"[1] This argument is made by many who promote canned curriculum, folks who don't seem to understand (or find it convenient to ignore) that teaching is about adapting everything you do to the needs of each class.

So now we have thousands of educators, some with multiple master's degrees (or even PhDs)—people who have dedicated their lives to the art of teaching—reduced to the role of an automaton. I've heard the same phrase, entirely independently, from several colleagues required to run their classes this way: "soul-crushing."

The more canned lesson plans catch on (and the increasingly profitable industry churning them out fairly well guarantees that they will), the more teachers will abandon their former "profession."

Solution

An article written for the National Association of Elementary School Principals quotes relevant research on commercial reading programs. The key findings are that "[T]he critical factor in successful reading instruction is not the program, but teacher quality"; "Programs that allow teachers to maintain some autonomy in literature selection, methods, and materials have been found to yield higher results in reading comprehension"; and "One program cannot meet the needs of all children. Teachers need to be trained and empowered to make decisions about how best to teach their students."[2]

Shocked, I tell you. Shocked!

Anthony Alvarado, a former New York City superintendent, expressed what one would hope was obvious: "[I]nstructional improvement depends heavily on people being willing to take initiative, to take risks, and take responsibility for themselves, for students and for each other."[3]

All this said, is there *any* place for canned curricula? Actually, yes.

As will be discussed, new teachers are often totally overwhelmed by the sheer volume of their responsibilities. Many rookies (and veterans for that matter) would be positively thrilled to have the option of turning to preplanned lessons in times of need.

But please note the word *option*.

If the script is mandated or must be followed to the letter, the only can it belongs in is the trash.

Notes

1   Justin Murphy, "Charter School Criticized over Lesson Script," *Rochester Democrat and Chronicle*, May 26, 2015, www.democratand chronicle.com/story/news/2015/05/26/rochester-prep-charter-school -lesson-script/27967605/.

2   Deborah Duncan-Owens, "Scripted Reading Programs: Fishing for Success," *Principal* 88, no. 3 (January-February, 2009): 26–29, doi:10.1057/9780230339729.0019.

3   Sarah Colt, "Do Scripted Lessons Work—Or Not?" *Making Schools Work with Hedrick Smith*, PBS, Sept. 2005, www.pbs.org/making schoolswork/sbs/sfa/lessons.html.

4

Trust Issues
Merit Pay and Accountability

!

Problem

There is nothing wrong with the idea of holding teachers accountable for doing their jobs well. But the current conversation about teacher accountability is doomed to failure because it rests on the faulty premise that teaching is only a science—and thus assessing educators is merely a matter of measuring the outputs (test scores) to evaluate the quality of the inputs (teachers). This is, at best, wishful thinking, even leaving aside the hot mess known as standardized testing and the fact that teachers work with different "raw material" in situations that can't be fairly compared.

The current advocates of teacher accountability make other problematic assumptions, too. For example, these advocates assume that their measurement tools measure what's important, and by implication that what the instruments don't measure isn't. They also discount the long-term effects good teachers have on their students, some of which don't show up on even the best-designed assessment tools. Over the course of my career, despite my best efforts, I've had students who did literally no work in my class. But more than one returned years later to apologize and to thank me for always treating them with respect—and to assure me that even though they never lifted a finger, they really did enjoy my teaching and that it made a difference in their lives. But as you can imagine, their test scores did not reflect well on me.

Let's imagine there is a reliable way to assess a teacher's effectiveness. Merit pay would still be a disaster. What's it for? Highest test scores? If so, few teachers will want to work with low achievers. But maybe it's for classes that show the most improvement? If so, teachers will avoid difficult content and student populations that are notoriously hard to improve. Whatever the case, do we want teachers shopping for the most lucrative students and designing their lessons with an eye toward profitability? Do we want to deal with parents who insist their children be placed in the most "meritorious" teachers' rooms? Do we want teachers competing with one another for the good graces of the merit pay dispenser? What will the environment be like when, inevitably, popular but undeserving teachers receive the extra pay? The number of worms in the can is countless, and it is impossible to imagine any actual benefits coming to fruition.

Among those educators fortunate enough to avoid merit pay regimes, many are still held "accountable" in unreasonable ways. Often teachers are primarily evaluated based on standardized test scores, which means it's not their students, colleagues, supervisors, or community assessing them, but for-profit corporations—with tools that are continually being proven unreliable. (Recently, a poet discovered two of her pieces included in the Texas state assessment. She couldn't answer the questions about them.[1])

The cult of standardized testing puts intense pressure on many teachers to drop what inspires both them and their students to "teach to the test." But, as reported in *Education Week* in 2011, "A blue-ribbon committee of the National Academies of Science" found that "nearly a decade of America's test-based accountability systems, from 'adequate yearly progress' to high school exit exams, has shown little to no positive effect overall on learning and insufficient safeguards against gaming the system . . ."[2]

In other news, the National Education Association (NEA) reports that nearly half of all teachers have considered leaving the profession specifically because of the current obsession with standardized testing.[3] And a study conducted by the *Annals of Depression and Anxiety* found that 44 percent of teachers have higher than normal anxiety.[4]

Even when standardized tests are not of primary concern, teachers are frequently required to prove their worth via "drive-by" evaluation. This happens when a district official with a checklist drops in to pass judgment upon a teacher after a single forty-five-minute observation (often much shorter) and frequently based on superficial requirements (Are learning targets on the board? Is the agenda for the day clearly visible? Is there a "Word Wall"?) It's not uncommon for such evaluators to have no knowledge of what came before the lesson or what will follow, and no information about the history of the students in the room. A colleague of mine, as a brand-spanking-new intern, was given sole possession of a Drama class midyear, following a string of subs after the original teacher resigned. She was given no scripts and no books—no plans of any sort. And no help. The class was full of seniors who did not need the class credit and had no interest in being there. You may not be surprised to hear that the class her evaluator observed did not go well. Completely ignorant of the unreasonable circumstances my colleague was dealing with, the evaluator's primary feedback afterward was to ask whether teaching was really what she wanted to do with her life.

Nor is it uncommon for such assessments to be made by a supervisor who wasn't even born when the teacher under review began their career—or who has never taught a day in their life. A seasoned teacher I know was taken to task by a young district evaluator who popped into her classroom unannounced—because he disapproved of reading aloud to students. He was in the room for a total of about ten minutes.

In the best cases, when (direct) supervisors have all the information necessary to make rational judgments—such as the details about the teacher's goals, their training, the students involved, etc.—they often have little time to make use of it. In real life, administrators have onerous caseloads requiring them to observe dozens of teachers multiple times, which often involve both pre- and postconferencing. Naturally, this frequently results in cursory evaluations.

Solution

The sad irony of the teacher accountability debate is that in every school, even without the benefit of data, the students, parents, staff, and administration all know who the great teachers are, who the average teachers are, and whether there are any who need to get on with their lives' work.

In my experience, aggregated student data is rarely instructive, at least the kind of aggregated data I've seen. For example, teachers are frequently asked to assess their effectiveness on the basis of a comparison between student scores in consecutive years, and they are then potentially made to alter their instruction as a result. Schools sometimes make sweeping decisions based on such information. Setting aside whether such scores actually indicate good teaching, every teacher knows that comparing how one class performed against the previous year is silly since they are made up of different students. Even if more reasonable data is used to compare a group to itself in consecutive years (data I've rarely seen), it's hard to say whether improved results indicate better instruction or increased student maturity. And regardless of what kind of data it is, teachers often don't receive it until *after* the academic year has ended, rendering it useless for making changes during the time such changes would be useful.

This is all not to say that statistics are useless. Obviously, a good teacher generates their own data, but timely, targeted, and comprehensible results from district/department assessments can be very valuable. The bottom line here is that if we continue to embrace sloppy science that reduces a multivariate issue (student success) to a single factor (teachers), we'll only continue to stifle the former while alienating the latter.

I realize that in this day and age the following solution will never be considered. But it's a solution that treats teachers as the scientist-artists they are and respects that the good they do is difficult to measure both in the short and long term.

If I were the boss, I would evaluate Mr. Slater via a series of simple questions: Are his learning targets/goals in line with those established by the district and his department? Are the pedagogical methods he is using to meet those goals among those considered effective practice for this situation? If not, what are his explanations of his methods? What are his own (self-selected) professional goals, and how is he progressing toward them? Do students, parents, and colleagues generally consider Mr. Slater a good teacher? What are my own observations of Mr. Slater as an educator?

If I am satisfied with the answers to these questions, Mr. Slater will receive a positive review, *regardless* of his students' standardized test scores. I will then look at that kind of data—assuming what is tested is valid. If significant discrepancies with colleagues' results are apparent, I would discuss possible reasons and potential adjustments. (In my Badge system, I'd, of course, want to know at what rate the badges are being earned.)

But given all the complexities involved, if we were serious about gauging teacher effectiveness, doing so *would be somebody's job.*

There would be an expert in every building who does nothing but observe, critique, and mentor teachers and whose role would also include speaking with all stakeholders (students, parents, colleagues, and administrators) about each teacher so that each year the evaluator could build a complete picture to assist them in helping educators grow as professionals.

However hard it is for some to swallow, here is the truth: all that can be fairly assessed is whether teachers are practicing their art in good faith—which means they employ thoughtful strategies to engage a maximum number of students in activities that promote their learning of the curriculum. There are just too many variables that account for student failure to blame it on teachers who are doing all that can be expected of them. To deny this is dishonest.

A simple accountability system, one that respects teachers, would attract more and better teachers to the profession. Such a system would not drive them away like the kind that insults them by implying they are responsible for factors everyone knows are well beyond their control. And surely that would lead to better results, no matter how you define them.

Al Ramirez, professor in the Department of Leadership, Research, and Foundations at the University of Colorado, Colorado Springs, sums up the challenge: "Policymakers should be careful about what they choose to reward—because they'll most likely get it."[5]

Notes

1   Sarah Holbrook, "I Can't Answer These Texas Standardized Test Questions About My Own Poems," *Huffington Post*, January 4, 2017, http://www.huffingtonpost.com/entry/standardized-tests-are-so-bad -i-cant-answer-these_us_586d5517e4b0c3539e80c341.

2   Sarah D. Sparks, "Panel Finds Few Learning Gains from Testing Movement," *Education Week* 30, no. 33 (May 26, 2011), http://www .edweek.org/ew/articles/2011/05/26/33academy.h30.html.

3 Tim Walker, "NEA Survey: Nearly Half of Teachers Consider Leaving Profession Due to Standardized Testing," *NEA Today*, November 2, 2014, neatoday.org/2014/11/02/nea-survey-nearly-half-of-teachers-consider-leaving-profession-due-to-standardized-testing-2/.

4 G. B. Gonçalves, "Assessment of Stress, Depressive, and Anxiety Symptoms in Teachers in the Public Education Network," *Annals of Depression and Anxiety* 2, no. 3 (2015): 1–6, http://austinpublishinggroup.com/depression-anxiety/download.php?file=fulltext/depression-v2-id1051.pdf.

5 Al Ramirez, "Merit Pay Misfires," *The Effective Educator* 68, no. 4 (December 2010/January 2011): 55–58, www.ascd.org/publications/educational-leadership/dec10/vol68/num04/merit-pay-misfires.aspx.

5

Job Security
The Tenure Debate

Problem

As I mentioned (and will mention again), teachers are fleeing the profession. Consequently, school districts are getting increasingly desperate to fill positions. Some are offering "signing bonuses," as if a onetime payment of $500 or $1,000 will suddenly render the job palatable.

At the same time, there are relentless attacks on arguably the only truly attractive perk of the career left: job security. Forget for a moment the wide range of critical benefits tenure secures, which includes, but is not limited to, protecting teachers from being fired for strictly personal, political, or budget-related reasons. If we aren't offering teachers competitive salaries, social respect, or actual job satisfaction—*and then we remove tenure*—what on earth is left to tempt *anyone* to take this job?

All that said, it would be disingenuous not to acknowledge that there are some ineffective teachers, even downright terrible teachers, who somehow, year after year, keep their jobs. Then there are the unions that sometimes seem more concerned with defending such teachers instead of making sure students get the best instruction possible. But *that* said, the size of this problem is grossly exaggerated by opponents of tenure—and of teachers and of public education—who seem to believe that there is a reservoir of better teachers waiting to save the day when the bad ones are purged.

Regardless, the problem is not tenure or unions going to absurd lengths to retain ineffective teachers (a recent Wellesley College study's title sums it up: "The Myth of Unions' Overprotection of Bad Teachers").[1] Tenure does not and never has meant a teacher cannot be fired. It only means they cannot be fired without due process. Every school district has a clearly defined process for principals to follow once they identify a stinker. It involves taking every possible step to help the teacher to improve, but it eventually gives a principal the power to terminate.

Solution

If this process is too cumbersome or convoluted to ever result in the firing of incompetent teachers, then school districts and teachers' unions must agree to improve it. In my opinion, it's simply a matter of will. The National Bureau of Economic Research released a study by Brian A. Jacob about terminations in the Chicago Public Schools after 2004 rules gave principals the power to fire teachers essentially at will. Jacob found that "[M]any principals—including those in some of the worst performing schools in the district—did not dismiss any teachers despite how easy it was under the new policy." He concluded that factors such as teacher supply and social norms might have been more responsible for the retention of teachers who warrant dismissal than has been previously recognized.[2] Thus we need to rethink our reflexive blaming of everyone's favorite scapegoat: unions.

If the will to remove bad teachers does not exist, perhaps state or federal intervention is necessary to enforce it.

Notes

1   Eunice S. Han, "The Myth of Unions' Overprotection of Bad Teachers: Evidence from the District-Teacher Matched Panel Data on Teacher Turnover," Feb 27, 2016, 1–62, http://haveyouheardblog.com/wp-content/uploads/2016/07/Han_Teacher_dismissal_Feb_16.pdf.
2   Brian Jacob, "Do Principals Fire the Worst Teachers?" Center for Local, State, and Urban Policy, University of Michigan Ford School, February 2010, closup.umich.edu/working-papers/20/do-principals-fire-the-worst-teachers/.

6

Sage on the Stage vs. Guide on the Side
Student-Centered Education

Problem

It is now generally accepted that students fair better when given a "voice"—that is, some level of decision-making power which encourages them to take ownership of their learning. This might or might not include influence over their curriculum, but it certainly involves the chance to make interest-based choices within it. (Yes, this is an obvious direct conflict with canned curricula and an obsession with standardized testing.) A 2014 study conducted by Hanover Research found, among other benefits, that "personalized learning, which frequently involves elements predicated on student choice, is considered an effective intervention for increasing student persistence rates."[1]

This approach, more commonly called Student-Centered Learning, involves lots of open-ended questions, group collaboration, and hands-on activities, as well as frequent self-reflection and goal-setting. It shifts the primary responsibility for knowledge-making to the student, so the teacher no longer spends all their time lecturing.

That is, they no longer dispense knowledge like a "sage on a stage," but rather they become more like a coach or a "guide on the side" who creates learning tasks that are engaging to get the ball rolling—and then makes themselves available to help active learners when they need it.

This is all well and good. In fact, giving students some level of control over their learning is at the very heart of all we do in gifted education. Personally, I almost never lecture. It's rare that I stand in front of the room even to give directions for more than a few minutes at a time.

The problem is that Student-Centered instruction is now practically a religion. We've reached the point where a teacher who wants to share a lecture for even fifteen minutes (and—*gasp*!—require their students to take notes) might be well-advised to lock the door and close the blinds. We've reached the point where twelve-year-olds are expected to run their own literary discussions so they can make their personal meaning from texts without "interference" from the "sage" (who can only stand by wishing one of them somehow had the background knowledge to unpack that complicated symbolism they've never been exposed to before). We are now in thrall to the notion that "passively" received knowledge is useless, if not some sort of affront.

This is especially strange since we are ostensibly preparing our students for college, where much of their learning will come via lectures. As philosophy professor Keith Parsons wrote in his *Message to My Freshman Students*: "Lecture, we are told, is an ineffective strategy for reaching today's young people, whose attention span is measured in nanoseconds . . . Hogwash. You need to learn to listen. The kind of listening you need to learn is not passive absorption, like watching TV; it is critical listening. Critical listening means that you are not just hearing but thinking about what you are hearing. Critical listening questions and evaluates what is being said and seeks key concepts and unifying themes. Your high school curriculum would have served you better had it focused more on developing your listening skills rather than drilling you on test-taking."[2]

A related problem is that in some cases the idea of Student-*Centered* Learning is misunderstood as Student-*Directed* Learning. In such cases, teachers essentially abdicate responsibility for doing their jobs by requiring students to teach each other with minimal guidance or support.

And Student-Centeredness is spilling out of the classroom. Advocates now want students to have a voice in how schools are run, including on issues considerably beyond the prom theme. For example, the 2014 Massachusetts Educator Evaluation Framework included student evaluations.[3] I've even come across advice on how to involve students in the teacher-hiring process.

Does respecting student voices promote a shared sense of purpose? Absolutely. Are there students in every single school whose energy and input might be harnessed for all kinds of educational benefits? Of course. But shared leadership is not the same as inclusive leadership. The first implies giving constituents equal shares of one's authority. The second involves listening to their concerns before exercising the power to make final decisions.

Moving complex institutions forward requires a captain with vision—and the power to steer the ship.

Solution

No fancy or clever solution is required here: choose the middle way! Student-Centered teaching methods are wonderful motivators, but they must be seen for what they are: effective tools among many others. And if you think teachers have no role to play other than as cheerleaders and problem-solvers or that the logical extension of the Student-Centered movement is that teachers and administrators must reject their own expertise and authority, you have thrown the baby out with the bathwater.

Notes

1   "Impact of Student Choice and Personalized Learning," Hanover Research, November 2014, doi:10.5040/9781472541406.ch-015.
2   Keith M. Parsons, "Message to My Freshman Students," *Huffington Post*, May 14, 2015, www.huffingtonpost.com/keith-m-parsons/message -to-my-freshman-st_b_7275016.html.
3   Massachusetts Department of Elementary and Secondary Education, "Quick Reference Guide: Student and Staff Feedback," *Educator Effectiveness* (July 2014): 1–2, http://www.doe.mass.edu/edeval/resources /QRG-Feedback.pdf.

7

The Customer Is Always Right

Students as Clients

Problem

Lately, it has become common practice for schools to survey their students about "school climate." This is wise, as staff and students can have very different perceptions of the environment in which they teach and learn. But I find such surveys can be emblematic of a troublesome shift at the heart of what makes education a less and less appealing profession to so many teachers. Specifically, surveys like one from New Jersey[1] ask students many questions about the influence and attitudes of teachers and peers, but none which imply that the survey subject themselves have a role in creating their school's climate. There are no questions, for example, about whether they feel education is important, or that they are responsible for their own learning, or for respecting peers and teachers, etc. Teachers and administrators should, of course, do everything in their power to promote the success of their students, but they alone do not create a school's climate.

This is just one example, but it's indicative of a cultural shift, perhaps best exemplified by colleges that now literally view their students as clients they must compete to please. In such an atmosphere, the character and comportment of students are considered irrelevant in the assessment of their teachers. Often hiring, firing, and tenure decisions at universities rely heavily on student ratings, despite the fact that, according to a study published by the Department of Statistics at Berkeley, "there is strong evidence that student responses to questions of 'effectiveness' do not measure teaching effectiveness."[2]

It is acknowledged that discussions of student disengagement and misbehavior are minefields riddled with stereotyping, bias, and even racism. Even so, it cannot be denied that the result of our student-as-client orientation is a culture in which educators are routinely blamed for causes of student failure that are mostly (and sometimes entirely) beyond their control. This is a culture that raises the individual to the level of a tyrant by insisting that disruptive students have more right to remain in a class they destroy than the rest of the students have to study in a learning environment free of distractions. A Special Ed paraeducator (which is an uncertified but supervised school employee) shared with me that he nearly lost his job for putting a hand on an out-of-control student wreaking havoc in his class. That's also just one example, of course, but consider that teachers in Allentown, Pennsylvania, recently declared that "disruptive students run the schools."[3]

This is also a culture in which parents assume the teacher is lying about an incident at school, not their ten-year-old. And one in which, all too often, administrators do not support their teachers in the face of attacks by students and parents.

Solution

I hope that you don't misunderstand me here. There are some teachers who cannot handle classroom management, who are bullies, and who lack the sensitivity of an anvil. I am a proponent of thoughtful interventions implemented for students who struggle with academics and behavior. I have been part of amazing, heartwarming transformations. But it seems to me that most decisions in K–12 education are made, first and foremost, with fear of lawsuits in mind. And while obviously the law is there to protect vulnerable students, the overly litigious atmosphere actually backfires, as teachers often avoid confronting difficult situations for fear of being sued. Most will no longer allow themselves to be alone with a student, especially one of the opposite sex, for fear of career-ending accusations of sexual assault. Principal Marguerite McNeely noted the following in a survey reported by *Education World:* "Teachers and other staff members often restrain from hugs, compassion the students are in so much need of, due to the fact someone might charge them with harassment." And this should be no surprise given that, as Principal Jim Jordan noted in the same report, "many parents are looking for something to sue about. They are looking for just one small slip-up . . . If they think they can get enough to get an out-of-court settlement, they file the suit."[4]

We might consider a law requiring parents to pay legal costs if their suits are found to be frivolous. But regardless, we must recognize that when teachers feel powerless to maintain an environment conducive to doing their jobs, they won't want the job.

Notes

1 State of New Jersey, Department of Education, "School Climate Survey," 2012, http://www.state.nj.us/education/students/safety/behavior/njscs/NJSCS_ES_Student_Q.pdf.

2 Philip B. Stark and Richard Freishtat, "An Evaluation of Course Evaluations," *ScienceOpen Research* (September 29, 2014): 1–26, doi: 10.14293/S2199-1006.1.SOR-EDU.AOFRQA.v1.

3 Jacqueline Palochko, "Allentown Teachers Speak Out: Disruptive Students Run the Schools," *The Morning Call*, November 17, 2015,

www.mcall.com/news/local/allentown/mc-allentown-schools
-teachers-students-violence-20151117-story.html.

4   Gary Hopkins, "Education World: Has the Threat of Lawsuits Changed
Our Schools?" Education World, September 28, 2004, www.education
world.com/a_admin/admin/admin371.shtml.

8

The Money Pit
Professional Development

Problem

One never-ending challenge faced by school administrators is bringing new teachers up to speed on established school- and district-wide programs, training staff on new initiatives, and making sure everyone keeps up with required continuing education throughout their careers. And while all of that is both reasonable and necessary, most teachers typically dread anything that passes under the name "Professional Development," or PD. Billions of dollars are spent on it every year, yet most teachers consider it useless—worse than useless, actually, since they usually have to miss instructional time (and prepare sub plans) to attend it. One study deemed these annual expenditures "largely a waste."[1]

Because most of the time *we're doing it wrong.*

Ironically, PD is typically delivered in a way completely antithetical to what teachers are taught makes for good instruction, that is, via long, lecture-style presentations. Despite the expectation that teachers differentiate their curricula for students at various skill levels, PD rarely does so for them. Thus, educators frequently find themselves suffering through training they've either already had, don't need, or that does not pertain to them at all. It is no exaggeration to say that in my nearly twenty years in education, I've attended probably a dozen PD sessions on cultural awareness that conveyed identical information.

Further, teachers are subjected to so many new concepts every year that they simply can't absorb them all, whether they are good or bad. And it's not uncommon that when wonderful new ideas are rolled out and everyone is properly trained to implement them, accountability is entirely absent—so only those supremely motivated to embrace them actually follow through.

Finally, it must be recognized that teachers' days are rarely structured in ways that promote the development of an adult-learning culture. There is virtually no time to debrief, reflect, consult, brainstorm, or even to simply commiserate with colleagues. Some schools address this issue with Professional Learning Communities, or PLCs, which are groups of teachers who meet regularly to discuss data and experiment with ways to improve student outcomes. But while PLCs can be transformative, they are more often than not merely one more requirement that overburdened teachers have to slog through.

Solution

A colleague of mine shared that she's been told by different administrators on more than one occasion that the reason teachers are always assigned PD on planning days (rather than given unencumbered time to get their work done) is that they simply aren't trusted to use the time well. I find that both offensive and depressing. Teachers are considered notoriously rude as an audience, but I'm not sure any group of professionals has more of its time wasted.

All that said, it is acknowledged that general PDs are necessary when administrators need to implement district-wide initiatives. Fortunately, researchers know what is required to make such undertakings successful: a clear purpose; shared language; teacher input; relevant, hands-on activities; accountability; and strong leadership that promotes a positive atmosphere.[2] But even if PDs are run well, such initiatives must be kept to a reasonable, achievable number, and however complicated the logistics may be to bring new hires on board, teachers who've received a particular training should never be required to sit through it again. Regarding more targeted initiatives, conference-style PDs—wherein attendees select from among many offerings—are a giant step in the right direction, but all possible efforts must be made to provide teachers with options they actually find valuable.

But here's an even better idea.

In every school, there is a vast wealth of expertise that is usually completely untapped: master teachers. Let's discuss two ways they can be used.

First, inexperienced teachers could be encouraged to observe or be observed by master teachers during their prep, or free, periods. When this occurs, both should be awarded the continuing education credit required to keep teaching licenses valid—a requirement that often sends teachers out in search of the most convenient, least annoying PD they can find when it becomes necessary. Note that this would cost considerably less than billions of dollars in that it would cost . . . *absolutely nothing*. Why this isn't happening every day in every school is hard to fathom.

Second, willing master teachers could also receive stipends to sign up for intensive district-wide training, and thus there would be an expert in every school responsible, or at least able, to facilitate the kind of follow-through necessary to make any new plan stick.

Another fantastic but underutilized form of PD is called "Charrettes." These are gatherings similar to medical "Morbidity and

Mortality" meetings (during which doctors present examples of their mistakes to colleagues, who then advise those doctors on how the mistakes might have been avoided). In Charrettes, teachers present "works in progress" for feedback from colleagues, whose collective experience and wisdom are drawn on for advice.[3] Depending on the level of trust established in the group, teachers might also share higher-stakes challenges, like student discipline problems, work-life balance struggles, or past failures. If facilitated properly, the entire group develops as educators.

Both master-teacher mentors and Charrettes provide teachers with what they rarely get in any form of PD: *new ideas that directly address their individual practice.*

Notes

1   Lyndsey Layton, "Study: Billions of Dollars in Annual Teacher Training Is Largely a Waste," *Washington Post*, August 4, 2015, www.washingtonpost.com/local/education/study-billions-of-dollars-in-annual-teacher-training-is-largely-a-waste/2015/08/03/c4e1f322-39ff-11e5-9c2d-ed991d848c48_story.html.

2   Barbara R. Blackburn and Ronald Williamson, "Pressing Forward with Professional Development," *Principal Leadership* 10, no. 5 (January 2010): 68–70, accessed March 6, 2017, http://eric.ed.gov/?id=EJ894650.

3   "The Charrette Protocol," School Reform Initiative, accessed March 5, 2017, http://schoolreforminitiative.org/doc/charrette.pdf.

9

Size Matters
The Class Size Debate

❗ Problem

In all the squabbling about education, the class size debate is perhaps the biggest face-palm. There are, it seems, reputable studies that show class size has no measurable effect on student outcomes (to wit, a *Washington Post* article entitled: "Study: Class Size Doesn't Matter").[1] But there are also reputable studies that show it does (again, to wit, a *Washington Post* article entitled: "Class Size Matters a Lot, Research Shows").[2]

But no teacher on earth needs to read any study to know this issue requires no studies at all.

Actually, here's the only study you need, and it's super cheap, too: just survey your common sense on what will *eventually* happen if you load a teacher up with five or six classes of more than thirty-five students (some have more than forty these days).

See, it doesn't matter if Awesome Elvis pulls off stellar results with those numbers and Average Joe across the hall with half the amount does not—since that data would completely miss the point.

The results are in:

It's a few years later, and Elvis has left the building. Stellar results or not, he burned out, so he took his talents elsewhere. Average Joe might've developed into an awesome teacher who also got stellar results, but he quit too because he was labeled a failure. Actually, that's not true, because Average Joe had class sizes just as large as Awesome Elvis all along. If Joe didn't quit, he slogged through and is barely hanging on—or maybe he's gone cynical and now just phones it in, proving to teacher-bashers everywhere that teachers really don't care.

Solution

Researchers find that between 40 and 50 percent of all teachers quit before their fifth year.[3] To be fair, this oft-cited statistic is disputed. For example, a US Department of Education study found the number is closer to 20 percent.[4] But even if we agree that the accurate number is somewhere between 20 and 50 percent, it's a troubling trend. There is no arguing that many states are in crises. One such state is Nevada, where our governor recently released a Statement of Emergency to "address the urgent teacher shortage."[5]

This book is full of reasons for teachers fleeing the profession, but burnout is surely near the top of the list. Either we want to make teaching a desirable job that attracts the best educators—or we don't. Not many people get into teaching for the salary or the prospect of promotion or social esteem. The truth is we rely on those who "do it for the children." We might want to stop driving them away by, among many other ways, telling them utterly absurd things like how many students we cram into their classrooms ought to make no difference to them.[6]

Notes

1 Suzy Khimm, "Study: Class Size Doesn't Matter," *Washington Post*, January 28, 2012, www.washingtonpost.com/blogs/ezra-klein/post /study-class-size-doesnt-matter/2012/01/28/giqaaizayq_blog.html?utm _term=.85464bb19d11

2 Valerie Strauss, "Class Size Matters a Lot, Research Shows," *Washington Post*, February 24, 2014, www.washingtonpost.com/news/answer -sheet/wp/2014/02/24/class-size-matters-a-lot-research-shows/.

3 Richard Ingersoll, "Beginning Teacher Induction: What the Data Tell Us," *Phi Delta Kappan* 93, no. 8 (2012): 47–51, http://www.kappan magazine.org/content/93/8/47.

4 Lucinda Gray, et al., "Public School Teacher Attrition and Mobility in the First Five Years: Results from the First Through Fifth Waves of the 2007–08 Beginning Teacher Longitudinal Study," National Center for Education Statistics, April 2015, nces.ed.gov/pubs2015/2015337 .pdf.

5 "Sandoval Signs Emergency Regulation to Immediately Address Teacher Shortage," Nevada Government, February 5, 2016, gov.nv.gov /news-and-media/press/2016/sandoval-signs-emergency-regulation -to-immediately-address-teacher-shortage/.

6 In case you are wondering, classes can be too small. There is research confirming this, but most teachers will tell you without reading it that eighteen to twenty-two students is ideal.

10

Extreme Teaching
Differentiation

❗

Problem

The most powerful teaching addresses diverse learners by tapping into student interest, addressing individual learning needs, and delivering detailed feedback in a timely manner. Those are principles that should guide all teachers' practice. But the current political climate forces educators to take extreme, and ultimately counterproductive, positions on the extent to which all this is possible.

You see, teachers today must pledge allegiance to a radical version of an otherwise laudable goal called "inclusion," which calls for every student who could even theoretically function on any level in a classroom to be in that classroom—because to "exclude" anyone is somehow undemocratic, elitist, or discriminatory.[1] In some cases, this even means the inclusion of emotionally handicapped students in regular education classes, students utterly unable to function in such environments—regardless of their ability to comprehend the curriculum.

Since we *begin* from the premise that radical inclusion is "best practice," there is no way to proceed except from the assumption that teachers *must* be able to execute it effectively. And thus it's not unusual for English teachers, as I often did, to have students who read at the 3rd-grade level sitting alongside those who can read and comprehend a dissertation. To "differentiate" (or customize curriculum) in an "inclusive" classroom like this, they must prepare lessons appropriate for them both—and all those at other levels who require totally different material, too. If that alone doesn't strike you as ridiculous, consider that teachers are also expected to deliver all this content in various ways to accommodate different learning styles.

Effective educators have techniques for adapting their lessons to meet varying student needs, but to require their application in unreasonable situations guarantees one or more of the following: rapid burnout; doing "it all" but doing it poorly; and/or differentiating only when supervisors are around.

Solution

Recently, there has been pushback against the practice of designing lessons around personal learning styles by "thirty eminent academics from the worlds of neuroscience, education, and psychology," who found the strategy unsupported by research. They concluded that the very idea of personal learning styles is a "neuromyth" that wastes money and resources—and, furthermore, potentially harms students by encouraging a limited sense of their true capabilities.[2] The pushback against differentiation, in general, was perhaps most forcefully expressed by education consultant James R. Delisle in a 2015 article for *Education Week*. In the piece, he declares, for many of the reasons listed above, that "differentiation is a failure, a farce, and the ultimate educational joke played on countless educators and students."[3]

Students in one class might be engaged with all sorts of material for all kinds of reasons. And sometimes, when it is convenient and doesn't allow them to avoid areas of weakness repeatedly, they might be allowed to access curricula or show their learning via preferred modes. This is reasonable differentiation. But expecting teachers to create five, ten, or thirty-five variations of their lesson plans every day is absurd. And students who cannot handle anything close to the given grade level of instruction or maintain a functional degree of emotional maturity should not be in the same room with those who can.

Ultimately, the solution to this problem requires many actions, such as reducing class sizes so teachers can actually provide individualized feedback in a timely manner. Whatever the case, we must recognize that educators cannot be expected to preside over mini-utopias where everyone, no matter what their differences, lives and learns in perfect harmony.

Our obsession with differentiation (and our devotion to radical inclusion) is damaging to teachers and students alike, but those who suffer the most are learners with higher needs—on both ends of the spectrum—because they require unique instruction.

Notes

1   These same politics are partly responsible for the elimination of woodshop and other vocational classes because they imply not all children are destined for college. Yet those who actually work with students know such courses were all that kept some students in school. Similarly, our obsession with standardized testing and the resulting single-minded focus on preparing for them has led to the elimination of electives like art and music that were also lifelines for many less academically inclined students. Of course, budget cuts are part of this equation too.

2   Sally Weale, "Teachers Must Ditch 'Neuromyth' of Learning Styles, Say Scientists," *The Guardian*, March 12, 2017, accessed March 13,

2017, https://www.theguardian.com/education/2017/mar/13/teachers-neuromyth-learning-styles-scientists-neuroscience-education.

3   James R. Delisle, "Differentiation Doesn't Work," *Education Week*, January 6, 2015, www.edweek.org/ew/articles/2015/01/07/differentiation-doesnt-work.html.

11

When Fair Is Not Fair
Gifted and Talented Education

Problem

Just about no one has a hard time accepting the idea that a child who tests in the first percentile does not belong in a mainstream classroom. Yet many resist the idea that a child who tests in the ninety-ninth percentile does not either. But the fact is that according to some (admittedly debatable) estimates, upwards of 20 percent of all high school dropouts are gifted. This should tell you all you need to know about what the regular education program does for (or to) many of those students.

There are gifted children who are suffering in classrooms all over the nation; they are bored, out of place, depressed, and even suicidal.[1] If they are fortunate enough to have been identified as gifted and their teachers are required to differentiate for them, their lot is often no better for it. Very few regular education teachers have any training in gifted education, so they often "accommodate" gifted students by requiring them to do the original assignment, which is usually a painful waste of time—and then *more*. Or they make them tutor the slower learners in the class.

But more often than not, gifted students (identified or not) are allowed to skate by without ever being challenged—because every assignment they turn in, despite the fact they require no effort, is far and away better than their peers'. The result is gifted youth who never develop the capacity to work hard, putting them at risk for failing to live up to their potentials, at the very least. We see many students like this in our gifted middle school program. It is often a terrible shock for them to find that they are no longer the smartest one in the room, and many such students struggle mightily to develop the work habits required to tackle material that actually pushes them.

Solution

Research shows that gifted students learn differently.[2] They need a deeper, more rigorous curriculum, they need to experience it at a faster pace, and they must be given a chance to engage with it among like-minded peers. Unfortunately, many people are against the idea of giving the "smart kids" their own classes because they feel it's elitist, antidemocratic, or just unfair (though they have no such complaints about Special Education students).

Even some teachers oppose taking Gifted and Talented students out of regular education classes. They think gifted learners don't need any help, that they'll be fine on their own, or that removing them from mainstream classes hurts the students left behind by denying them role models—though studies show the opposite to be true. In fact, when gifted students leave regular classrooms, the remaining students rise up into the "space" left behind. As explained by noted experts in the field of gifted education, "[r]esearch indicates that students model their behavior on the behavior of others who are of similar ability." They go further in noting that gifted students often feel arrogant and thus reluctant to participate in heterogeneous classes, while the other students can be made to feel inferior.[3]

Other teachers resent having their best, most engaged pupils siphoned out of their rooms, lowering the overall level of discourse. And while that is likely a real phenomenon, it's hardly a reason to deny gifted students an education commensurate with their needs.

Fortunately, the pendulum is swinging in favor of gifted education, so more programs like the one I teach in, which allows gifted students to take their core classes with gifted peers, are likely to sprout up around the nation in the very near future.

Notes

1   Patricia A. Schuler, "Gifted Kids at Risk: Who's Listening?" Supporting Emotional Needs of the Gifted, September 14, 2012, http://sengifted .org/gifted-kids-at-risk-whos-listening/.
2   You can read a wealth of information about gifted education at the website for the National Association for Gifted Children at www .nagc.org/resources-publications/gifted-education-practices.
3   Ellen D. Fiedler, Richard E. Lange, and Susan Winebrenner, "The Concept of Grouping in Gifted Education in Search of Reality: Unraveling the Myths about Tracking, Ability Grouping, and the Gifted," *Roeper Review* 24, no. 3 (September 1993): 102–7, media .hoover.org/sites/default/files/documents/0817928723_85.pdf.

12

The Opposite of Success

A Bubble-Wrapped Generation

Problem

We now have several generations raised on well-intentioned but bad parenting advice—the essence of which is that the self-esteem of children is so fragile that it must be protected at all costs, lest they develop permanently debilitating inferiority complexes. The good idea in this line of thinking is that healthy self-esteem is a vital characteristic of psychologically healthy people. Where it went wrong was in the assumption that setbacks, struggles, and failures impede this development—when in fact they are indispensable to it (assuming they are not extreme). To put it another way: the self-esteem movement failed to understand that failure is not the opposite of success, but rather a necessary part of achieving it. This fundamental misunderstanding is responsible for the "Participation Trophy Culture" lamented by social critics like Ashley Merriman, coauthor of *Top Dog: The Science of Winning and Losing,* who argues that "Losing is good for you."[1]

This phenomenon has, not surprisingly, found its way into education. Teachers, especially in early grades, are often pressured not to let their students "fail," or even flounder. Teachers in all grades find "overparented" students in their rooms who are terrified of making mistakes and of taking risks associated with stretching—with learning. But who can blame them when they've been raised to avoid discomfort in all forms, or when they have no experience with failure as instructive?

The net result of all this is an unprecedented number of young men and women arriving for college entirely unequipped to deal with the challenges there. As reported by Penn State University's Center for Collegiate Mental Health, the use of psychiatric services on our nations' campuses is steadily rising.[2] No doubt there are myriad reasons for increased levels of anxiety and depression among college students, but it cannot help if before arriving they were shielded from stress at all costs.

Solution

First, schools should make every effort to educate parents on the effects of overparenting. This might involve sending literature home and hosting information-sharing sessions. Maybe we need a nation-wide public service announcement (PSA) campaign as well.

Second, we must create an atmosphere in every classroom that not only destigmatizes risk-taking and mistake-making but celebrates them. This involves explicitly addressing such things, but also more nuanced attention to subtle culture-shaping signals like praise. As Carol Dweck's seminal study proved, when students are praised for their intelligence, they begin to fear tackling further challenges—because they don't want to risk losing their status as "smart." But when students are commended for being hard workers, they'll give anything a go—because bad results do not invalidate such praise.[3]

Similarly, teachers must promote "growth mindset," another theory by Dweck which posits that people who view setbacks as beneficial are more likely to learn than those who see them as proof of permanent defects.[4] I myself can vouch for the transformative effects of establishing such a culture, as I've had many students write essays and reflection letters testifying to the fact that, because they came to see failures as helpful, they formed new attitudes about facing obstacles in their lives.

But even if a teacher successfully promotes such a climate, it will be undone if the grading system routinely punishes risk-taking.

Notes

1   Ashley Merryman, "Losing Is Good for You," *The New York Times*, September 24, 2013, www.nytimes.com/2013/09/25/opinion/losing-is-good-for-you.html?_r=0.

2   Penn State University's Center for Collegiate Mental Health, "Center for School Mental Health 2015 Annual Report," January 2015: 15–108, doi:10.1007/springerreference_69808.

3   Carol S. Dweck, "Caution—Praise Can Be Dangerous," *American Educator* 23, no. 1 (Spring 1999): 4–9, http://www.inner-cityarts.org/documents/resources/PraiseCanBeDangerousCarolDweck.pdf.

4   Note that this popular theory is rapidly becoming another example of a good idea gone bad as teachers are apparently overpraising students just for trying when they fail—unintentionally sending the message that trying is a good enough end in and of itself—and that succeeding (or at least improving) is not actually the goal.

13

Stay on Target
Helicopter Parents

Problem

The most extreme overparenters are referred to by teachers as "Helicopter Parents." They are notorious for micromanaging their children's lives: scheduling their free time down to the minute; choosing their friends; exaggerating their every "accomplishment"; and interfering in all aspects of their academic lives. (This trend is now being observed not only in high school and college but in *graduate* school.[1])

What having a "Helicopter Child" in the classroom means for a teacher is constant communication from mom or dad about every element of every assignment, receiving work that is often clearly the result of too much help at home, and—in the worst cases, when the parent is displeased—unending conflict. Helicopter Parents are certain their child is infallible, so any problems little Johnny experiences at school are both unacceptable and someone else's fault. (This willingness to attack and blame the teacher at all times is, of course, supported by the general cultural tendencies to avoid personal responsibility and to disrespect teachers.)

At times, Helicopter Parents will go so far as to bully teachers if that's what it takes to "protect" their child. Teachers of Helicopter Children (typically female teachers) are subject to aggressive behavior from parents on a regular basis, whether in the form of nasty emails or phone calls, threats of lawsuits, or, as in the case of a relative of mine, verbal attacks in the parking lot.

Most Helicopter Parents don't attempt to intimidate teachers, but they will go to extreme lengths to help their children avoid challenges. A colleague shared with me the story of one of her students who fell behind after battling leukemia. Despite the fact that her son was not in need of Special Education modifications for any learning disability, this mom successfully demanded that the Individualized Education Program (IEP) designed to help him catch up specify that if he received a 59 percent or lower in a class, the grade recorded on his transcript would be a C. If his grade was 60 to 69 percent, it would be a B, and 70 percent and up would be an A. Subsequently, he made the National Honor Society and received a scholarship based on his grades. This, of course, is grossly unfair to other students, but one also fears how such an "enabled" student will handle college classes that award grades that are actually earned.

Children of Helicopter Parents are fairly easy to recognize. They are functionally less mature than they ought to be, are terrified of making mistakes, need constant praise, and require mom or dad's input on and support for everything they do. Most troubling is that, according to one study, such overparenting results in "reduced child resilience, a sense of entitlement, child anxiety, reduced life skills, and an inadequate sense of responsibility or self-efficacy."[2] According to another study, overparenting results in high rates of anxiety and depression.[3]

Solution

Parental involvement in their children's education is not only a good thing, it's a fundamental necessity. However, many parents need a complete reorientation on the notion of failure. Simply put, they must allow their children to struggle and fail when the lessons of those struggles and failures need to be learned. They must see their role as making sure such lessons are learned, not to ensure their children never have to learn them. If a child's decisions are not likely to result in permanent damage, they should be subject to their natural consequences. Any educator or old-school parent can tell you—there is no better teacher.

Notes

1   Hara Estroff Marano, "Helicopter Parenting—It's Worse Than You Think," *Psychology Today*, January 31, 2014, www.psychologytoday .com/blog/nation-wimps/201401/helicopter-parenting-its-worse -you-think.

2   Judith Y. Locke, et al., "Can a Parent Do Too Much for Their Child? An Examination by Parenting Professionals of the Concept of Over-parenting," *Journal of Psychologists and Counsellors in Schools* 22, no. 2 (December 12, 2012): 249–65, doi: http://dx.doi.org/10.1017/jgc .2012.29.

3   "Intrusive Parents May Lead Children to Be Overly Self-Critical: NUS Study." National University of Singapore, June 21, 2016, news .nus.edu.sg/press-releases/10531-intrusive-parents-self-critical.

14

Going It Alone
Absent Parents

Problem

It should be noted that while the Helicopter Parenting/human bubble-wrapping phenomenon may be part of a larger cultural trend of infantilizing our children, as it pertains to our nation's schools, it is ultimately a middle-class and upper-middle-class problem. If our schools' biggest obstacle were *overly* involved parents, we'd be in a much better place. By far the larger problem is the vast number of parents who are totally *un*involved in their children's education: parents who do not answer calls from the school; who do not show up to parent-teacher meetings or school events; and parents who appear—at least to those with little understanding of this issue—not to care about their children's education.

Solution

The truth is that just about everyone cares about their children's education. The fact that some families want nothing to do with their children's schools, despite all appearances, does not prove otherwise.

So there's no sense blaming absent parents, even if their lack of support is a primary reason for their children's failure at school. We need, rather, to understand why they avoid schools. Some typical reasons are known: they are intimidated; they are embarrassed by their own lack of education; their experiences as children dealing with the school system were traumatizing; and/or they simply don't feel welcome. But to assume any of these is the case in any particular situation is problematic.

Parents in poverty are the largest group disengaged from their children's schools, but they are not a monolithic one. As Eric Jensen, author of *Teaching with Poverty in Mind*, points out, there are six types of poverty: situational (caused by crises); generational (in which at least two generations of a family were born into poverty); absolute (families literally surviving day-to-day); relative (families unable to achieve their community's standard-of-living); urban (poor families who suffer from uniquely urban stressors); and rural.[1] So it's a mistake for a school to attempt to engage such families without understanding their particular situations. As one study concludes, "[E]ven with the best of intentions, middle-class educators create and implement practices intended to serve low-income families without an assessment of community needs. Programs may be offered but go unattended without that assessment."[2]

But even with the relevant information, it can be a serious challenge to bring low-income families into the fold, especially when it comes to those enduring generational poverty. Donna M. Beegle, an expert in this area, found in a study of adults who surmounted generational poverty that "98 percent of them reported that education had little or no meaning in their early lives and simply was not important. For nearly all of them (92 percent), early education was just something they 'did' and never knew why."[3]

The bottom line here is that if schools really hope to bring disengaged families (of all sorts) into their orbit, they have to understand them. And then they have to be creative about what it might take to motivate their participation, which we will discuss in the next chapter.

Notes

1 Eric Jensen, "Chapter 1: Understanding the Nature of Poverty." Association for Supervision and Curriculum Development, 2009, www.ascd.org/publications/books/109074/chapters/understanding-the-nature-of-poverty.aspx.
2 Jane Graves Smith, "Parental Involvement in Education Among Low-Income Families: A Case Study," *The School Community Journal* 16, no. 1 (Spring-Summer 2006): 43–56, www.adi.org/journal/ss06/smithspring2006.pdf.
3 Donna M. Beegle, "Overcoming the Silence of Generational Poverty," *Talking Points* 15, no. 1 (2003): 11–20, www.washington.edu/omad/files/2013/03/overcoming-generational-poverty-article.pdf.

15

The Opportunity Gap
Poverty

Problem

In 1980, the bottom half of the US population earned 20 percent of the nation's wages. In 2014, it was 12.5 percent.[1] And now, over half of all public school students in America come from low-income families, qualifying them for Free and Reduced Lunch.[2] Government data released in 2015 estimated the number of homeless students at well over 1.3 *million*.[3] The impact of economic inequality on our ability to provide quality education for all has been nothing less than profound.

Prime examples of how poverty impacts learning include the following: children from low-income families are often exposed to a far less rich vocabulary than their peers with professional-class parents;[4] they tend to lack role models;[5] they might be hungry and consequently unable to concentrate at school;[6] chronic stress can impede the development of their executive functioning skills;[7] and their unstable or unpredictable home lives may lead to depression.[8] As famed psychologist Abraham Maslow explained, *in 1943,* people whose basic needs are unmet are not able to pursue higher ones, like education—certainly not up to their capabilities.

As if these hurdles at home aren't enough, poor students are much more likely to attend schools that lack adequate resources. Those experiencing homelessness often have the additional burden of constantly starting over at new schools (even though the wonderful McKinney–Vento Homeless Assistance Act provides protection and funds to combat this problem).

This all adds up to what educators call the "Opportunity Gap," defined by expert Linda Darling-Hammond as the "disparity in access to quality schools and the resources needed for all children to be academically successful." She considers the Opportunity Gap "the greatest crisis facing America's schools."[9] And she's right.

But those who point to poverty as a (frequently) insurmountable hurdle to learning are attacked on several fronts. First, they're told that they are simply wrong because poor students in other countries do better on international tests. But as the Economic Policy Institute points out, "Because social class inequality is greater in the United States than in any of the countries with which we can reasonably be compared, the relative performance of US adolescents is better than it appears . . ."[10] Not to mention many of these comparison countries offer universal pre-K.

But, anyway, it doesn't matter. Too many poor students do miserably *here.*

Second, they are accused of *contributing* to the problem by excusing failure—though they do nothing of the sort. Until we face the facts about the devastating effects poverty has on education, we won't begin to offer the kind of interventions that students living in poverty actually need.

As noted, researchers have found many causes for the academic struggles of low-income students, but common sense alone is all that's needed to know that the major offensive waged by the "no excuses" crowd against the Opportunity Gap—"raising standards" and testing more—is guaranteed to fail. A trio of trailblazers in the field of educational justice put it best in an op-ed for the *Washington*

Post, wherein they defended the wisdom of at-risk students opting out of high-stakes tests: "We now know students cannot be tested out of poverty."[11]

When students are tired, hungry, or traumatized, and when their families are in distress or their neighborhoods are dangerous places—all talk of standards is just that: talk. As Professor Pedro Noguera, one of these trailblazers, argues, we must end this "either-or debate."[12] We can have high expectations for students in poverty *while* working to eliminate the obstacles to their reaching them.

Solution

The phrase "Opportunity Gap" replaced "Achievement Gap" because the latter implied that what's holding disadvantaged students back are teachers rather than egregious income inequality. Recognizing that the causes of this crisis lie outside the education system was absolutely critical, but schools must nevertheless play a role in helping solve it.

This means attacking the problem as one of poverty, not standards.

First, the outrageous and deplorable conditions in schools where poverty is most pronounced must be remedied. Yesterday.

Second, we need to do whatever it takes to motivate great teachers to take jobs in low-income schools—great teachers who understand how to create a caring and encouraging environment for students living in poverty. Such educators are desperately needed to (among many other things) help students cope with their disadvantages by fostering resilience skills. They are best able to, for example, "Help youths identify a 'strength' or 'buried treasure' that will be a 'ticket out of the . . . high-risk environment' and help them find a 'guardian angel' who can make a difference by providing needed supports."[13] And since it seems that students are more likely to view a teacher who shares a background with them as a role model,[14] we must make sure they have them.

Next, educators must take an "all-of-the-above" approach to bringing low-income parents and guardians into their schools (recognizing that families in poverty are often nontraditional in structure and that underemployed caretakers often cannot attend school events during the times they are typically scheduled). For starters, this requires finding out what days and hours such families are available to come to school events and then facilitating both transportation and child care to make attendance possible. Schools should be given the resources and permission to provide incentives for such participation, like hygiene supplies and meals or take-home food bags.

Finally, schools must try in every way possible to become larger parts of their communities. This might include creating safe zones for students after school, opening food and clothes banks, or supplying space for lawyers and health professionals willing to donate hours. Innovative public-private school-housing partnerships show promise for keeping homeless and other low-income students in place by, in some cases, providing vouchers to help cover the cost of housing—vouchers that are gradually reduced as the family moves toward self-sufficiency.[15]

But we know the Opportunity Gap starts at birth (as a "Readiness Gap") when many poor children are deprived of all sorts advantages when it comes to health care, emotional security, and exposure to educational experiences. As a result, they all too often arrive at Kindergarten woefully behind their more fortunate peers in many ways that they rarely overcome. As the Economic Policy Institute points out, "[S]ocioeconomic status, or social class, is the single largest predictor of early education gaps."[16]

This means, if we truly want to address this critical issue of equity, it must be a national priority to impact low-income children before they reach school age. This might involve offering free universal preschool, but it will definitely require a coordinated effort among everyone with the power to affect poor children's exposure to (for starters) early literacy, from pediatricians to social workers to law enforcement—even to private corporations, who also have a stake in ensuring that our nation's children all have the chance to reach their highest potentials. Examples of powerful interventions include First Book, "a nonprofit social enterprise that provides new books, learning materials, and other essentials to children in need." According to their website, the organization has "distributed more than 160 million books and educational resources to programs and schools serving children from low-income families."[17] In Nevada, we have the nonprofit organization 1,000 Books Before Kindergarten, which is dedicated to promoting reading to newborns, infants, and toddlers.

Bottom line: anyone and everyone willing and able must be on board. If there's no real "war on poverty," we must launch a genuine assault on preventable readiness gaps.

I don't have an exhaustive list of solutions to this problem for a very good reason: the best solutions will involve *asking* each community what will incentivize and enable it to work in partnership with its schools.[18] We know that great things can happen when this is accomplished. For example, Academic Parent-Teacher Teams, which are designed for parents and teachers to discuss data, goals, and how best they can support learning together, have been used to drive dramatic turnarounds in both achievement and culture in some of the lowest-performing schools in the country.[19]

But whatever we do, we must bear in mind Darling-Hammond's concise articulation of what this all comes down to: "The opportunity to learn—the necessary resources, the curriculum opportunities, the quality teachers—that affluent students have, is what determines what people can do in life."[20]

Notes

1   Patricia Cohen, "A Bigger Economic Pie, but a Smaller Slice for Half
    of the U.S.," *The New York Times*, Deccember 6, 2016, accessed
    December 8, 2016, https://www.nytimes.com/2016/12/06/business
    /economy/a-bigger-economic-pie-but-a-smaller-slice-for-half-of
    -the-us.html.

2   "A New Majority Research Bulletin: Low Income Students Now a
    Majority in the Nation's Public Schools," Southern Education Foun-
    dation, accessed December 7, 2016, https://eric.ed.gov/?id=ED555829.

3   Department of Education, "Total Number of Homeless Students En-
    rolled in LEAs with or without McKinney–Vento Subgrants—Total:
    2013–14," ED Data Express, accessed March 16, 2017, https://ed
    dataexpress.ed.gov/data-element-explorer.cfm/tab/data/deid/5353/sort
    /idown/.

4   Betty Hart and Todd R. Risley, *Meaningful Differences in the Ev-
    eryday Experience of Young American Children* (Baltimore, MD:
    Paul H. Brookes Publishing Company, 1995), www.leadersproject
    .org/2013/03/17/meaningful-differences-in-the-everyday-experience
    -of-young-american-children.

5   Eric Jensen, "How Poverty Affects Classroom Engagement," *Faces
    of Poverty* 70, no. 8 (May 2013): 24–30, www.ascd.org/publications
    /educational-leadership/may13/vol70/num08/how-poverty-affects
    -classroom-engagement.aspx.

6   NoKidHungry.org, "Hunger in Our Schools 2015," https://www
    .americandairy.com/_resources/documents/no-kid-hungry-hungerin
    ourschoolsreport-2015.pdf.

7   Paul Tough, "How Kids Learn Resilience," *The Atlantic*, May 16,
    2016, accessed April 16, 2017, https://www.theatlantic.com/magazine
    /archive/2016/06/how-kids-really-succeed/480744/.

8   Melissa Tracy, et al., "What Explains the Relation between Family
    Poverty and Childhood Depressive Symptoms?" *Journal of Psychiatric
    Research* 42, no. 14 (October 2008): 1163–75, www.ncbi.nlm.nih.gov
    /pmc/articles/pmc2672881/.

9   Linda Darling-Hammond, "Opportunity Gap—Talking Points,"
    Schott Foundation for Public Education, accessed December 6, 2016,
    http://schottfoundation.org/issues/opportunity-gap/talking-points.

10 Martin Carnoy and Richard Rothstein, "What Do International Tests
    Really Show about U.S. Student Performance?" Economic Policy

Institute, January 28, 2013, www.epi.org/publication/us-student
-performance-testing/.

11 Valerie Strauss, "'We Now Know Students Cannot Be Tested out
of Poverty,'" *The Washington Post*, June 3, 2015, accessed December 6, 2016, https://www.washingtonpost.com/news/answer-sheet
/wp/2015/06/03/we-now-know-students-cannot-be-tested-out-of-
poverty/.

12 Pedro Noguera, "Accept It: Poverty Hurts Learning," *In Motion Magazine*, September 20, 2010, accessed December 6, 2016. http://www
.inmotionmagazine.com/er/pn_acceptit10.html

13 Donald Meichenbaum, "How Educators Can Nurture Resilience In
High-Risk Children And Their Families," Teachsafeschools.org, accessed April 15, 2017, http://www.teachsafeschools.org/resilience.pdf.

14 Elizabeth Stockslager, "Supporting Minority Students Through
Mentoring: Best Practices for Formal Mentoring Programs" (master's
thesis, 2013, Paper 1856), pdfs.semanticscholar.org/3cfd/b38a603e
27cc902d0ffbc6a286538ab587d6.pdf.

15 Evie Blad, "K–12, Housing Partner to Aid Homeless Students," *Education Week*, March 9, 2014, accessed April 15, 2017, http://www
.edweek.org/ew/articles/2014/12/10/housing-partnership-aids-home
less-students.html.

16 Emma Garcia, "Inequalities at the Starting Gate: Cognitive and Noncognitive Skills Gaps between 2010–2011 Kindergarten Classmates,"
Economic Policy Institute, June 17, 2015, www.epi.org/publication/
inequalities-at-the-starting-gate-cognitive-and-noncognitive-gaps-in
-the-2010-2011-kindergarten-class/.

17 "Equal Access to Quality Education for Children in Need," First
Book, accessed April 15, 2017, http://firstbook.org/the-need/.

18 I hate to say this, but heartwarming stories about how teachers
make personal connections with troubled students that totally alter
the course of their lives, turning them from, say, gangbangers into
honor-roll recipients, may actually be counter-productive in terms of
spurring the kind of change we need. This is because, while such
transformative relationships are always possible (and are at the heart
of what teaching is meant to be), the implication always seems to be
that *if every teacher only cared like that one, all students could succeed*—
when in fact what such rare stories should make people think is, *if all
teachers were free to make those kinds of connections with students . . .*

19 Department of Education, "A New Framework: Improving Family Engagement," *ED.gov Blog*, December 20, 2012, accessed December 8, 2016, http://blog.ed.gov/2012/12/a-new-framework-improving-family-engagement/.

20 Linda Darling-Hammond, "Opportunity Gap—Talking Points," Schott Foundation for Public Education, accessed December 6, 2016, http://schottfoundation.org/issues/opportunity-gap/talking-points.

16

Deadlines and Do-Overs
Proficiency, Growth, and Grades

Problem

The utter unreliability of grading in K–12 education is an open secret. It's a primary reason that standardized tests in one form or another will never go away. You won't often find two teachers in the same hall whose grading methods align, let alone in two different schools, districts, or states. There are teachers who give copious extra credit, allowing students who didn't actually learn much of the course content to salvage their grades; there are teachers whose grades include points for compliance, for example, dressing down for physical education or bringing in forms promptly; there are teachers who weigh homework so heavily that a student who doesn't do it cannot pass their class regardless of their performance on assessments; and there are teachers who award grades for growth rather than mastery, so that a student who improves dramatically yet still cannot demonstrate minimal skills might receive an A. And on and on.

Proficiency-based (or Mastery-based or Competency-based) grading attempts to fix this mess. In essence, its purpose is to separate academic from nonacademic behaviors so that grades reflect only one thing: the skill level a student has attained. Teachers must explicitly identify an achievable number of learning targets, and course grades must be based solely on final assessments of them. This means a student who declines to do homework or in-class assignments (or who doesn't even show up to class on a regular basis) but who receives *A*s on these assessments must receive an *A* in the course. It's hard to argue that any of that work was necessary if a student can hit the targets without doing any of it.

In some ways, the Proficiency-based model effectively addresses fundamental problems with typical grading systems: it clarifies the true purpose of coursework (practice for assessments); it emphasizes the demonstration of acquired knowledge and skills; and it refuses to misinform students about their actual level of competency.

But it's also often impractical and even counterproductive because it assumes that "nonacademic" behaviors like reliability, cooperation, and follow-through are not fundamentally important for students to develop in school, even though they are certainly required everywhere else in life.[1] For example, in a purely Proficiency-based school, deadlines are not enforceable, because turning in an assignment on time is a nonacademic behavior. Students are typically offered many, sometimes virtually unlimited, opportunities to retake assessments because, it is argued, the goal is to learn, not to learn on a timeline and because different people learn at different rates.

I worked in a Proficiency-based high school. Many of our students came to us because they could not succeed in their former, more traditional, schools. They had very challenging lives. They had tough home situations. They had after-school jobs—frequently two. Many of them *needed* second, third, fourth, and sometimes fifth chances. They needed a school willing to wait until they were ready and able to commit to their learning. For them, this model was a godsend.

But as proof positive that there is no single solution to our biggest problems in education, for the many other more typical students there, it was nothing of the sort. It actually *untaught* good habits. When they discovered homework was optional, they stopped doing it. When they learned they were always free to retake exams, they studied when it was convenient. When they found that deadlines weren't really deadlines, they submitted their work only when time finally ran out—which, believe it or not, initially didn't happen *until the following year.* As you might imagine, teachers were utterly swamped with assignments, projects, and do-over test-requests at the last possible minute. Each year, our well-meaning administration had to walk these policies back further and further so we could do our jobs.

Solution

There is a larger question at play here, perhaps the largest: What's the purpose of public education? Is it to impart measurable academic skills? To prepare students for the workforce? To teach the type of critical thinking strategies needed by an active citizenry in a healthy democracy? To promote personal growth? To mold children into adults capable of living harmoniously in a diverse society?

Short answer: yes.

But let's be clear: the bedrock responsibility of public schools is unquestionably the teaching of academic skills. Any school that fails to do so fails its students. But the fact that educators can and must do so much more should warn us away from a single-minded focus on assessing skill attainment. Besides, the simple fact of the matter is that nonacademic behaviors sometimes simply cannot be separated from academic behaviors, if only for practical reasons like those described above.

That said, insofar as it *is* possible, academic and nonacademic behaviors *should* be separated. When they can't be, it must be made abundantly clear to a student what part of a grade reflects their academic performance and what part reflects something else.

Other insights from Proficiency-based advocates should be taken into account as well, but implemented prudently . . .

First, students should not be required to complete work they've already mastered. Ideally, this would apply to entire courses. This wastes their time and contributes to academic disengagement.

Second, emphasizing final products is wise. Doing so gives students the freedom to struggle with and even fail assignments designed to prepare them for assessments. Does anyone hold it against an actor or musician who stinks up their rehearsals but nails the live performance? But we must remember that in education we are dealing with young people: de-emphasizing the importance of practice *too* much invites them to dismiss it entirely.

Finally, students should be allowed to redo some projects and/or retake some exams (although one hopes a do-over test is not identical to the first). Such opportunities can be very motivating—but only when they are limited. If there is no consequence for abusing second chances (for example, we cap redo or retest grades at 75 percent), students are encouraged to take advantage of the system, which undermines its purpose. It's a popular school mantra that "it's never too late to learn." Maybe so, but sometimes it's too late to get the grade you want.

While we should do our best to calibrate grading practices between instructors, the truth is there simply is no realistic way to ensure that an A means precisely the same thing in every class. Better to focus more on strategies which ensure that grades are meaningful in every class. Some superior reporting methods are well-known, for example, narrative assessments (prose descriptions of student performance that eschew letter grades). But they are unreasonable to expect given the average teaching load.

For a better solution, I must turn again to the Badge system, however unlikely it is ever to be implemented. I believe it actually solves the Growth vs. Proficiency debate because it allows educators to use the best of both approaches (as the scientist-artists they are). Great teachers understand that sometimes Growth-based grades are needed to encourage struggling learners. It's a true art to know exactly when and how to award them. Doing so in the Badge system would not ultimately misinform students about their skills, though, because, in the *end,* all that would matter is whether the badge was earned—which should be a much more objective determination. In other words, teachers would be trusted to do whatever they think best to move their students toward mastery.

In the absence of such a model, I am an advocate of grading systems that include a traditional academic grade but also one for "Work Ethic" and "Behavior" or "Life Skills." (Badges could even come with such information appended). Having these three strands of data, separated as much as possible, is very informative. If for example, I'm a parent of two C students and one's report card includes low Work Ethic scores while the other's is very high, I would react very differently. But such details would only exist if schools consider nonacademic behaviors important.

Note

1   That said, homework, if not necessary for a particular student, should be either dropped for them or adjusted. If a student can master a class without attending it, they belong in a more challenging one.

17

Introverts vs. Extroverts

Group Work

Problem

Just a generation or two ago, students did not regularly collaborate on assignments. They typically sat at their desks, did their work, and then handed it in. This is no longer the case. But as is so often the case when we become enamored of new ideas, we take them too far. Many teachers now hesitate to plan a lesson without incorporating some form of cooperative learning.

Of course, students derive many benefits from well-designed group assignments. Research shows that cooperative learning leads to greater efforts to achieve, better relationships, and increased psychological health.[1]

I'm a big fan of group work. It's central to much of what we do in our Gifted and Talented program.

So what's the problem?

Well, first there's the fact that group assignments are often not well-designed and thus create more conflict than collaboration (hence the popular meme: "What I Learned from Group Work in School: Trust No One"). Or they are not preceded by any form of independent thinking and thus devolve into what some call "igno-rance sharing."

Furthermore, as Diana Senechal, author of *Republic of Noise: The Loss of Solitude in Schools and Culture,* writes, on teams, "one group member tends to take control and the thoughts of those who are quieter or don't fit in socially are disregarded."[2] I would argue this is often the case even in well-designed group tasks. But even when groups are equitable and effective, if participating in them is always required, a clear message is sent to quieter students, the introverts: there is something wrong with preferring to work alone.

This message is troublesome because, as Susan Cain, leader of the "Quiet Revolution"[3] asserts, introversion is not a problem (un-less it's extreme—but then extreme extroversion is a problem, too). She argues that, in fact, introverts have valuable contributions to make to society. Only, they need time alone to make them. Teach-ing introverts, explicitly or implicitly, that their very nature is fun-damentally flawed is educational malpractice.

Solution

To be clear, all students—introverts, extroverts, and those who are combinations of both—need to develop collaborative skills. Natu-rally, this may be much harder for introverts than extroverts. But every student must also be able to commit sustained, focused efforts to solitary tasks and to engage in thoughtful reflection. These skills tend to be harder for extroverts.

The answer? Teachers must continue to create effective, struc-tured collaborative opportunities for students on a regular basis, which often requires the facilitation of team- and empathy-building activities first. But it should not be only "worksheets" or other obvious solo tasks that are usually done by individuals. There must be times when students who wish to do creative, long-term projects alone are permitted to do so. Teachers should also seek and use strategies that accommodate both types of learners when appropriate, such as Think/Write/Pair Share, for example.

But most important, it must be made absolutely clear to students that both introverted and extroverted personalities are to be respected and valued.

Notes

1 David W. Johnson and Roger T. Johnson, "What Is Cooperative Learning?" Cooperative Learning Institute, www.co-operation.org/what-is-cooperative-learning/.
2 Holly Welham, "Group Work Is Overused in Schools, and in My Experience It Stifles Good Ideas," *The Guardian*, September 21, 2014, www.theguardian.com/teacher-network/teacher-blog/2014/sep/21/group-work-school-quiet-reflection.
3 Susan Cain, *Quiet Revolution*, www.quietrev.com/author/susan-cain/.

18

Spring Spheres
Diversity Education

Problem

Perhaps you think schools have no business promoting "values." And of course, when it comes to strictly religious values, you are absolutely correct. But consider that many classrooms are full of students who do not have what we might call the social or civic values which make it possible to teach them. If a teacher finds their pupils don't respect one another's right to, for example, speak without interruption, then the teacher has to teach that value so they can get on with the business of delivering the curriculum. Similarly, if students do not value each other's cultural differences or, worse, scorn them, then schools have no choice but to teach (at the very least) tolerance so the institution can function.

The problem with promoting an atmosphere of social inclusion is not in the intention, but rather often in the execution, which in many places is dreadful because educators may lack cultural competency[1] and thus fail to understand what integrates and what alienates marginalized students—and some teachers just don't care.

Some more culturally sensitive educators do make efforts, but these are often unintentionally token gestures. For example, a school may schedule a "Diversity Week" during which it dedicates time each day to study minority groups that otherwise receive little attention. That's the better version. Often the best a school can do is a "Culture Fair," typically an evening of cultural "show and tell" when various "cultural" artifacts are shared and ethnic foods are served. In my opinion, such efforts are prone to backfire because they invite the kind of stereotypes people pick up from exposure to superficial cultural differences.

Other efforts fail because educators make either ignorant or empty gestures toward "diversity." An uncorroborated story circulated the internet recently about a Seattle teacher allowing a teen volunteer to hand out Easter eggs to her class, but only after instructing her to call them "Spring Spheres," a linguistic maneuver she evidently thought would render Christian holiday treats culturally inclusive. Whether or not this actually happened, it captures the depressing dearth of understanding many teachers have about these issues.

I myself have witnessed a teacher who thought that instructing her students how to say "Merry Christmas" in ten languages promoted diversity and another who thought having students ask Santa for whatever gift they wanted for "whatever holiday they celebrated" was culturally sensitive. I've heard teachers argue with near violence that festooning a school with Christmas trees, Santas, and Rudolphs is *absolutely not exclusionary* because they are seasonal decorations—which *are not religious symbols.* As if a Jewish or Muslim child makes any distinction between a cross, a Christmas tree, and an Easter egg (or, for that matter, a Spring Sphere).

For many reasons—including conscious antipathy toward church and state separation, fury at "political correctness" run amok, and simple insensitivity to others—some educators find it difficult to recognize that it is their responsibility to maintain an atmosphere that doesn't marginalize non-mainstream groups. But even harder for some to accept is that this is not enough: it is also their responsibility to maintain an atmosphere that doesn't make such groups feel like tolerated—or even welcome—guests.

Solution

Any school dedicated to creating a truly inclusive environment must promote acceptance of cultural differences and demand tolerance of them. This can only be accomplished if the message is embedded in everything the school does. There are never any separate celebrations, except perhaps to place special emphasis. That is rule number one.

Second, any school that genuinely cares to discover how its traditionally marginalized students feel there *should ask them*. In my experience, school climate surveys rarely drill down to this level. They do not track students' race, gender, or religion, and they don't ask the kind of questions that would generate the information required to assess how inclusive the school actually is. Of course, if a school is prepared to ask such questions, it better be prepared to deal with the answers.

Note

1   For a primer on the five elements of cultural competency, visit the National Education Association at www.nea.org/tools/30402.htm.

19

The Buddy System
Modern Anti-Bullying Programs

!

Problem

According to the US government, nearly one in three students report being bullied.[1] There might be no more pernicious problem to stamp out in our schools than bullying. On the positive side, awareness of its prevalence, its permutations, and the irreparable damage it can cause has increased exponentially in recent years.[2] On the downside, there is little evidence that any of the anti-bullying programs we spend millions of dollars on work.

At best, researchers report modest results, but at least one study found that "bullying prevention had a negative effect on peer victimization."[3] The authors theorized that anti-bullying programs might actually teach bullies how to bully better.[4]

It would be impossible here to analyze the details of all anti-bullying campaigns used across the country, but it's fair to say that many feature disturbing advice. This includes, in one form or another, a message that it's the victims' responsibility to diffuse the situation—whether via firm talk, humor, or otherwise—and that it's *never* acceptable to physically fight back. Furthermore, it's not uncommon for victims to be required to participate in mediation sessions where refusing to accept coerced apologies from their bullies is not an option. The Bullies2Buddies program, for example, is founded on a "Golden Rule": love your bullies.[5] In my opinion, such advice bullies the bullied.

And then of course there are those who suggest that all the hand-wringing about bullying is further proof of how we've gone soft as a society. They argue that the real world is full of bullies, so kids have to "toughen up" to deal with them on their own. No doubt these are folks who themselves toughened up by dealing with bullies on their own. Those who wound up scarred, damaged, or broken may beg to differ with this approach.

Shouldn't we ensure that children reach adulthood intact so that they can engage with the world, however they find it, as fully functioning individuals?[6]

Solution

Once again, we must begin with an admission that schools cannot solve all of society's problems. In this case, they cannot "fix" every bully by transforming them into buddies through education.

That said, schools have to take an all-of-the-above approach here as well. If there are programs proven to yield good results, they should try them. But like the intimately connected need to promote tolerance and the acceptance of diversity, it cannot involve token efforts.

That said, let's get one thing straight: while it's not a school's place to promote violent self-defense, it is outrageous to equate it with unprovoked violence. Unless one is prepared to argue that force is never called for, under any conceivable circumstance—including, say, in the case of a bully actually murdering someone—then we already agree that there comes a time when physical self-defense is justified. And that means the conversation is about where that line is, not whether there is a line. Any anti-bullying program that does not include explicit recognition of this should be out of the question. In some cases, a school might be justified in suspending both a bully and a victim who fought back, but they better not be equal punishments. The bully must be made to understand that violent retaliation is a natural and predictable consequence of bullying, and while the victim is not to be congratulated (perhaps), he must be made to feel understood.

Three further observations: first, a recognition I rarely hear in regard to "bully-proofing" schools is that we are dealing with, for the most part, children whose brains are literally not fully developed—so "teaching" bullies not to bully is a questionable strategy at best; second, one does not require a psychology degree to know that bullies often bring their issues to school from home—so expecting to undo this damage without changing what's happening outside of school seems like wishful thinking; and third, everyone knows most bullying at school occurs when no one is watching, for example in bathrooms, hallways, etc.[7] Since that is one issue schools actually can impact, it stands to reason that it ought to be the basis of prevention.

Here's my solution: schools should be positively packed with (vetted) members of the community. There should be multiple adults, perhaps retired folks, wandering every hall, loitering on every stairwell, hanging out under all the bleachers—and, yes, walking in and out of restrooms. This is a way to bring school and community together, and this is how you make sure there simply are no opportunities for bullies to bully.[8]

Notes

1   US Department of Health and Human Services, "Facts about Bullying," October 14, 2014, www.stopbullying.gov/news/media/facts/#listing.

2   US Department of Health and Human Services, "Effects of Bullying," last updated September 12, 2017, www.stopbullying.gov/at-risk/effects/.

3   Seokjin Jeong and Byung Hyun Lee, "A Multilevel Examination of Peer Victimization and Bullying Preventions in Schools," *Journal of Criminology* 2013: 1–10, doi:10.1155/2013/735397.

4   Allie Bidwell, "Study: Anti-Bullying Programs May Have Opposite Effect," *US News & World Report*, September 13, 2013, accessed November 24, 2016, http://www.usnews.com/news/articles/2013/09/13/study-anti-bullying-programs-may-have-opposite-effect.

5   Izzy Kalman, "The True Meaning of the Golden Rule: Love Your Bullies," Bullies2Buddies, February 20, 2010, bullies2buddies.com/the-true-meaning-of-the-golden-rule-love-your-bullies/.

6   I can feel you pointing back to chapter 12 and the "Bubble-Wrapped Generation," and I would worry very much that this sort of approach would be misused, that is, to protect students from every conceivable slight and hurt feeling. But please keep in mind that we are talking about bullying here only, and that means real persecution. Adults need not supervise or police every interaction—they simply need to be around because their mere presence changes how children and adolescents behave. Is there really a good reason that schools operate so apart from their communities?

7   "Where Is Bullying Most Common?" NoBullying.com, December 22, 2015, nobullying.com/where-is-bullying-most-common/.

8   Cyberbullying is another subject entirely.

20

A Blank Slate
The Writing Crisis

❗ Problem

Every fall, college instructors nationwide renew their complaint that the latest batch of students who've shown up in their classrooms cannot write. Not cannot write *well*—cannot meet even minimum college-level expectations. Consequently, many colleges have had to add remedial writing courses to bring freshmen up to basic competency. (According to the National Center for Education Statistics, "In 2011–12, about one-third of all first- and second-year bachelor's degree students—29 percent of those at public four-year institutions and 41 percent of those at public two-year institutions—reported having ever taken remedial courses."[1])

We have reached this sad state of affairs for a few reasons.

Here's what I know is required to teach students to write well: 1) provide many opportunities to take on meaningful writing tasks; 2) give timely, personalized feedback on rough drafts—and the chance to revise them; and 3) supply instructive critique on final drafts for use on the next task.

This sort of program is virtually impossible in the current K–12 environment.

There used to be actual writing courses offered in many schools, but they turned into "Language Arts" classes so English teachers could teach writing and reading, in the same amount of time, of course. Many school districts have gone even further, transforming Language Arts teachers into "Humanities" teachers so they could also be responsible for the social studies curriculum—again, often in the same amount of time. So combine an uncoverable amount of material with unreasonable class loads—and let's also sprinkle in high-stakes assessments that rarely include writing, since it is too expensive to assess—and the predictable result? Hardly anyone teaches writing anymore. Certainly not in the way described above.

But no school district official will admit that writing can't be properly taught under present circumstances since they evidently can't be changed. So we hear all kinds of cockamamie claims about students being able to learn from writing only paragraphs, or without getting teacher feedback, or with only input from each other. And, predictably, de-professionalizing web-based programs are being purchased that can supposedly "read" student essays and automatically critique them.

I would also argue that in many cases where writing has been taught for the last decade or so, much damage has been done by "best practices." The first was the result of another pendulum overswing, this one in the form of a pushback against strict enforcement of essay forms, specifically the dreaded "five-paragraph essay." It seems too many teachers required too many students to write nothing else until a rebellion occurred. But that rebellion, naturally, went too far. The message was that requiring conformity to any preexisting type of composition is stifling, and to assign a five-paragraph essay of any kind is to crush a child's creative soul. And so there is at least one generation of students with no knowledge whatsoever that time-tested structures exist which help shape certain types of written expression.

The second equally problematic issue arose as pressure increased on teachers to engage in "cross-curricular" lesson planning, which, for example, requires English teachers to make sure their assignments fit together like pieces in a puzzle with one or more of the other subjects. This is not a bad idea. It can be very effective to have students, for example, write a persuasive letter to the editor about cleaning up the local environment while they are studying it in Science. *But here's the most important thing I know about teaching writing:* a real passion for it is ignited in students when they are free to find their own subjects. And that is simply not possible when every writing task must be yoked to something already in the curriculum.

Solution

We teach writing the way it must be taught in our Gifted and Talented program. Our students are exposed to models of varying quality and given time to draft in class on a regular basis. They write two essays per quarter (one to three pages, depending on the grade level). On one, they receive feedback on drafts and finals, and on the other (an essay test), they only get feedback on the final. But to give you an overall idea of what this entails, it takes me ten minutes to provide feedback per essay, and I have in a given year between 85 and 125 students. And that's ten minutes because I'm rather quick about it; fifteen minutes is probably more standard. (I did the math for you: one set of essays is over twenty-four hours.) I lose entire weekends every quarter doing this, which are—if you're not getting this—entirely unpaid. I don't do this because I'm a saint. I just don't know how else to get my job done.

I'm often asked why I've never pursued educational leadership, at least in English/Language Arts. The primary reason is that I have another career (author), but the other is that I could never tell anyone else that the only way to effectively do their job is to work this way (even though it is).

Reasonably sized Writing courses must be added to K–12 programs, or English teachers' class loads must be significantly reduced.[2] At the very least, administrators should find a way to provide time during the school week for English teachers to read and provide feedback on writing tasks.

But on the issue of *what* to teach, we must get past our silly and damaging vilification of teaching "formulas." In fact, what we must teach—to beginners—are *forms,* which, as pointed out by screenwriting guru Robert McKee, exist because they have proven to be effective over time. Our Gifted and Talented middle school students learn to write nine types of essays over three years. But by the end of 8th grade, they understand that these forms are not actually formulas because they are malleable, that they can be combined or reshaped—for example, you might use narrative and compare/contrast strategies to formulate an argument. Our students leave confident that they have the basic tools needed to tackle more complicated writing tasks in creative ways.

My former high school juniors, who arrived to my class never having learned a single way to shape any type of essay, couldn't believe such structures existed. Their gratitude for my sharing blueprints of various essay types was such that I had to make sure they didn't think I invented them. But the main reason they embraced learning them so enthusiastically was that they were given the freedom to write about whatever they wished. Consequently, I was often deeply moved by their work. Of course, some students wrote about frivolous topics, such as the relative merits of various boy bands, but more often than not they took on deeply personal ones. I vividly recall the high school senior's research essay on what returning veterans might expect to face when they reintegrate with their families, a subject she chose because her brother was soon to return from active duty to his wife and child. And the essay about the ways victims of a disease the author's mother had contracted could best cope with what was coming. Just recently, I sent an 8th grader's beautiful cause-and-effect essay about dealing with her grandfather's dementia to a local publication for seniors, who immediately published it. The student gave me a thank-you note in which she wrote that she'd previously never imagined she could be a "good writer," and that the experience of getting published for the first time provided her with "a light at the end of the tunnel" of her grief. This kind of thing rarely happens when students are forced to write on topics their teacher assigns.

When asked what makes my writing instruction work, I'm almost embarrassed by how few tricks I have up my sleeve: Expose students to various writing tasks, help them practice the skills necessary to execute them well, then allow them to use those skills to express themselves freely.

Notes

1   Xianglei Chen, "Remedial Coursetaking at U.S. Public 2- and 4-Year Institutions: Scope, Experience, and Outcomes Statistical Analysis Report," Institute of Education Science, September 2016, nces .ed.gov/pubs2016/2016405.pdf.

2   Another idea is to give English teachers regular "feedback days" out of the classroom to assess useful writing tasks. This is a great stop-gap idea because it doesn't require structural change (though it does cost money). In the end, it still risks burnout.

21

Students for Sale
Advertising in Schools

Problem

The more cash-strapped school districts are forced to struggle for resources, the more tempting it is for them to turn to easy solutions, like taking money from corporations in exchange for access to their students. As a result, children all over the country are being plied with freebies like coupons and branded school supplies and exposed to ads on vending machines, walls, lockers, and buses. Then there is Channel One, a program shown in schools to upwards of five million students every day, according to its website.[1] The consumer advocacy group Commercial Alert describes Channel One as "a company that delivers two minutes of advertising and ten minutes of 'news,' banter, and fluff to captive audiences."[2] Many districts also sell exclusive "pouring rights" to soft drink corporations, even in the face of current childhood obesity statistics. One district recently agreed to include a Target logo on its elementary school supply list for $9,000.[3]

What's the harm?

First, note that every single ad in a school has the implicit endorsement of the school. Second, consider that children, teens especially, are a coveted market by the billion-dollar advertising industry for a reason. As noted by the MediaSmarts organization, this is not only because teens have disposable income or because they wield considerable influence over their parents' buying choices—it's because they are the adult buyers of the future.[4]

Modern marketing, it must be acknowledged, does not exist to disseminate information, but rather to create and influence consumers, and we know how persuadable children and teens can be. Forget for a moment that parents might object to having their children, in a captive environment, exposed to products they disapprove of (fast food, for example[5])—the ads in schools are carefully created to undermine critical thinking skills, the teaching of which is supposed to be one of the central purposes of education.

Advertising accomplishes this by playing on students' emotions, and often the same emotions schools find to be the source of problems they otherwise try very hard to solve. For example, many ads exploit the common teen fear of being left out, pressuring them to do what it takes to become "popular." The American Psychological Association notes that ads aimed at teens encourage them to "tie brand choices to their personal identity."[6] Is this what we want to be promoting in our schools?

And is the following scenario far-fetched?

A high school signs a million-dollar contract with a major soft drink company, which finances its new football stadium. A teacher in the school launches a Media Literacy Unit.[7] One of his students decides to research the questionable practices of the very corporation that now financially supports the school. He finds some highly disturbing information and publishes it on the project blog.

I hope I need not spell out how this story ends or what lesson the student learns from it. If it does seem far-fetched, consider the case of Michael Cameron, who in 1998 was suspended for wearing a Pepsi shirt on "Coke Day." His school didn't even have a contract with Coke but was rather attempting to win a local contest. As described in the *New York Times*, "The Coke contest offer[ed] $500 to the Columbia County school that [came] up with the most creative method of distributing promotional discount cards to students."[8]

Solution

Public schools are supposed to be one of the very few level playing fields in our society, even if it's only for our children. This means students must be treated equally, regardless of their races, religions, genders, sexual orientations, etc. But it also means that we must take pains to shield them from all the manipulative messages that assail them when they are virtually everywhere else. If companies actually care to support our schools, they are free to make charitable donations.

Notes

1   "What Is Channel One News?" Channel One, www.channelone.com /about-us/.
2   "Channel One," Commercial Alert, archive.commercialalert.org/issues /education/channel-one.
3   "Winston-Salem/Forsyth County School Supply Lists to Feature Target Logo," myfox8.com, July 30, 2013, myfox8.com/2013/07/30/winston -salemforsyth-county-school-supply-lists-to-feature-target-logo/.
4   "How Marketers Target Kids," MediaSmarts, mediasmarts.ca/mar keting-consumerism/how-marketers-target-kids.
5   According to the Campaign for a Commercial-Free Childhood, "67.2 percent of students are exposed to corporate advertising for foods of minimal nutritional value or foods high in fat and sugar in their schools." http://www.commercialfreechildhood.org/sites/default/files /schools.pdf.
6   American Psychological Association, "Driving Teen Egos—and Buying —through 'Branding'," *Monitor on Psychology* 35, no. 6 (June 2004), www.apa.org/monitor/jun04/driving.aspx.

7 Media Literacy is a course of study growing worldwide. It promotes teaching students, among other skills, the ability to critically assess media messages in terms of their purpose and persuasive strategies. For more information, visit https://medialiteracyproject.org/learn/media-literacy/.

8 The Associate Press, "A Pepsi Fan Is Punished in Coke's Backyard," *The New York Times,* March 26, 1998, www.nytimes.com/1998/03/26/business/the-media-business-a-pepsi-fan-is-punished-in-coke-s-backyard.html?_r=0.

22

The Coming Crisis
Teacher Shortages

Problem

If the fact that between 20 and 50 percent of new teachers don't make it to their fifth year doesn't alarm you, perhaps the declining enrollments in teacher training programs might. According to the Learning Policy Institute, "Between 2009 and 2014 the enrollment in teacher education programs dropped from 691,000 to 451,000, a 35 percent reduction," a problem compounded by the fact that "school enrollment is projected to increase by roughly three million students in the next decade."[1] It's difficult to find clear statistics on retirement rates, but most of the older teachers I know can't wait to get out of their classrooms. Those who have retired couldn't be more relieved—or less encouraging of others to enter their lifelong profession.

As discussed, there is a whole host of reasons for this, including general lack of respect, unmanageable workloads, increasing reliance on high-stakes testing, lack of autonomy, never-ending new initiatives, and rules that prevent teachers from controlling behavior in their own classrooms. Whatever the case, the growing teacher shortage has resulted in the hiring of uncertified instructors. When the problem is addressed with licensed teachers, they are often given assignments outside of their certifications (this practice even has its own acronym, TOOF, for "Teaching Out of Field"). Current evidence of the prevalence of this practice is lacking, but a survey in 2000 revealed that "nationally, one out of four secondary classes in core academic subjects (24 percent) are assigned to a teacher lacking even a college minor in the subject being taught."[2]

I have a friend who recently received his English certification. He was hired to teach English in a high school but only for half of his assignment. The other half was in Special Education, an area in which he had absolutely no training or experience. He was left to sink or swim in that capacity, and within a few months, he was relieved of the position. He went on to resign completely before the end of October and now despairs of ever teaching again.

Teacher shortages will eventually precipitate a national crisis and scandal that will finally force people, especially those who consider education to be a career choice for slackers and freeloaders, to finally confront the reasons so few people want this job anymore.[3]

Solution

There are two issues here: How do we attract new teachers to the profession, and once we do that, how do we keep them there? Let's start with the second.

It's well-known among teachers that the newest hire frequently gets the least desirable assignments. A relative of mine, as a newly minted, bright-eyed and bushy-tailed twenty-four-year-old educa-tor, was assigned six classes at a suburban high school: two Junior History sections, two Junior AP History classes, and two sections of Freshman Global Studies. She was responsible for 165 students, the second heaviest load in the school.

While seniority must confer tangible benefits on dedicated employees, we cannot saddle our most inexperienced teachers with crushing burdens.

Furthermore, new teachers cannot be left to fend for themselves. This relative was assigned no mentor to help her acclimate, and the curricular support she received consisted of a pile of old textbooks and worksheets, the likes of which she was trained to avoid. During that first year, she was constantly sick, lost weight, and suffered chronic stress.

Are you surprised she didn't return for year two?

Schools must provide new teachers with, at the very least, master teacher mentors, help with classroom management, access to a range of up-to-date curriculum materials, and the chance to meet with other new teachers with whom they can discuss their experiences. But note that none of these interventions address the core reasons new teachers quit. At best, they help them cope with an often overwhelming job.

One initiative aimed at attracting new teachers to the profession is called Alternative Route to Licensure (ARL), which allows anyone with a BA who can pass a standardized test to complete required coursework while teaching on a provisional license. Such policies can attract mature, midcareer folks who are interested in teaching but who can't afford to quit their jobs to enroll in a full-time licensure program. But, as above, ARL does nothing to make the conditions such recruits will find once they enter the classroom more tolerable. It's yet to be seen how teachers certified this way are faring.

The simple truth is that new teachers will not enter or remain in the field in meaningful numbers until we make the career more attractive. That means making teachers' salaries competitive. The National Education Association reports that teachers' starting salaries are far below those who start in comparable careers and that the longer they teach, the greater this gap becomes.[4] That is not a formula for attracting or retaining talent.

But given the unlikelihood of increased salaries materializing anytime soon, we need to seriously consider combinations of other inducements, like forgiveness of college debt for new teachers who reach their fifth or tenth year in the profession. Or offering extremely attractive home loans. Such plans would, of course, upset "old" teachers, and that cannot be left unaddressed. But when it comes to recruiting teachers to inner city and rural schools—these kinds of ideas could work right away.

A related issue is Last in First Out (LIFO) policies, which stipulate that the latest hires are let go first when budget cuts require reductions in force. These cannot simply be dispensed with since the promise of job security is one of the few remaining attractions of a teaching career. That said, waving LIFO in hard-to-staff urban and rural schools (by guaranteeing new hires' jobs for a certain number of years) might be a creative way to entice great teachers to work in them.

Notes

1   Leib Sutcher, et al., "A Coming Crisis in Teaching? Teacher Supply, Demand, and Shortages in the U.S.," Learning Policy Institute, September 15, 2016, learningpolicyinstitute.org/product/coming-crisis -teaching.
2   Craig D. Jerald and Richard Ingersoll, "All Talk No Action: Putting an End to Out-Of-Field Teaching," *Education Trust*, August 1, 2002, repository.upenn.edu/cgi/viewcontent.cgi?article=1142&context =gse_pubs.
3   Or, in some cases, the particular job: a big part of the problem is a shortage of teachers willing to work in inner city or rural schools.
4   "Myths and Facts about Educator Pay," National Education Association, www.nea.org/home/12661.htm.

23

The Zombie Apocalypse

School Start Times

Problem

The zombie apocalypse is already upon us. Just poke your head into the average middle or high school where adolescents are required to be in class sometimes as early as 7:30 a.m. You'll see shuffling, semiconscious creatures with half-open eyes, some evidently with broken necks no longer able to hoist their heads up.

Sleep deprivation is a serious and widespread problem in American society, one that surely exacerbates our many chronic health issues. But adequate sleep is not a luxury—it's a necessity to maintain both physical and mental health. There are, of course, tremendous economic and social pressures that lead adults to forgo necessary sleep, but there is no good reason to foist a sleep-deprived lifestyle on our children.

Here's why: a growing body of research shows that sleep-deprived adolescents can't learn well, are unhealthy, make bad choices, drive dangerously, and generally don't develop to their full potentials.[1] And if that list isn't disturbing enough, *The Journal of Childhood Psychology and Psychiatry* recently published a study concluding that sleep-deprivation in teens is a risk factor for adult crime. It found that "Sleepy adolescents were more likely to be antisocial during adolescence, and were four and a half times more likely to commit a crime by age twenty-nine."[2]

Solution

This is not simply a matter of bedtimes.

Going to sleep at a reasonable hour is, of course, part of the solution, but before we propose any remedies, we need to understand that a teenager's inclination to stay up late and sleep late has "biological and physiological roots."[3] In other words, within reason, it's perfectly natural.

Unfortunately, recognizing this doesn't make finding a solution much easier. This is because school start times are not the way they are because anyone thinks they are good for . . . anyone. They are a matter of practicality (district transportation), access to extracurricular activities (more time for practice), and entrenched habit. It's impractical to imagine that sweeping changes will be made requiring later start times, but the American Psychological Association has proof that schools and districts across the country which have voluntarily switched to later start times have experienced multiple benefits, including a reduced number of disciplinary actions, decreased accidents involving students, and increased GPAs.[4]

I believe, at the very least, more schools and school districts should do the same so that additional evidence can be gathered. If the data becomes too overwhelming to ignore, change will spread.

Notes

1   For more information, visit www.startschoollater.net/why-change .html.

2   Adrian Raine and Peter H. Venables, "Adolescent Daytime Sleepiness as a Risk Factor for Adult Crime," *Journal of Child Psychology and Psychiatry* 58, no. 6 (June 2017): 728–35, doi: 10.1111/jcpp.12693.

3   "Later School Start Times Promote Adolescent Well-Being," The Children, Youth, & Families Office of the American Psychological Association, 2014, doi:10.4135/9781452276250.n236.

4   Ibid.

24

A Class Issue
Homework

!

Problem

Schools should think long and hard about their homework policies. Burdening students with too much, especially in the younger grades, can undermine everything educators hope to accomplish. But the idea of banning it altogether is misguided.

The real problem is that much of what goes under the name of homework is time-wasting busywork. And this fact no doubt accounts for why so many students and parents vehemently condemn it. Opponents also say it causes undue stress, strains families, and—bottom line—does not contribute to learning.

Useless homework deserves every bit of criticism it receives. Let's abolish it. But effective teachers who wish to prepare students for college know they cannot possibly hope to do so without requiring some work outside of class in the upper grades. English teachers are the first to scoff at the thought of teaching literature without asking students to read books at home—or of having them write substantial essays in class on a regular basis. It's interesting to note that one of the hottest "innovative" trends in education right now is the "Flipped Classroom,"[1] which frees teachers from instruction during class to answer questions as students engage with, rather than receive, content. This is accomplished by requiring students to watch videos or read information ahead of time. At home.

It is also pointed out that homework is a socioeconomic issue because only students with enough leisure time in their lives can successfully complete it—in other words, middle-class students. There is no disputing this observation, but neither is there disputing the observation that *college itself* is the very embodiment of middle-class values. Prohibiting the type of behavior (independent study) required for success in college for the students who would most benefit from access to it in the name of fairness seems paradoxical at best.

Solution

Homework should not be assigned unless it's absolutely necessary, and it's surely never necessary in Kindergarten. That's first. Second, it should be entirely clear to students why they need to do, or better complete, a given assignment at home. Third, grades associated with homework should be minimal relative to the final assessment it is meant to prepare students for. (If the homework is not preparation for the final assessment, it should be considered, by definition, not necessary.) Ideally, homework would not be graded at all, as the natural consequences of not doing it should teach powerful lessons. But as we've discussed, children often lack judgment and the ability to consider long-term consequences.

Also of critical importance is whether the curriculum is engaging. It's unrealistic to expect every course of study to inspire such enthusiasm that it spills over onto the homefront, but when students are interested in their work and when they have some choice in how to pursue it, they are much more willing to tackle it out of the classroom.

Finally, regarding students whose lives make it difficult for them to do homework, whether because they are required to be caretakers at home, have jobs, lack access to technology, or receive no family support—the answer is not depriving all other students of the benefits of reasonable amounts of well-conceived homework. Rather, educators must identify these students and put structures in place to help them succeed. This might mean providing an extra study hall or an after-school tutoring session, finding someone to donate a laptop, or working with parents, if it's possible, to support home study. What we can't do, or continue to do, is allow our understanding of disadvantages to harm those we wish to help.

Note

1 For a discussion of the pros and cons of the flipped classroom, see https://net.educause.edu/ir/library/pdf/eli7081.pdf.

25

Robbing Peter
School Choice

Problem

Proponents of school vouchers (essentially a coupon parents can put toward the tuition at a school of their choosing) claim they improve public schools by forcing them to compete for students.

Which makes no sense.

First, virtually nothing fundamental about public and private schools is comparable, so there is very little public schools can learn from how private schools operate. As a prime example, public schools are ridiculed for their poor handling of discipline. But what can they learn from a private school free to expel (or suspend or remove from class) students according to whatever set of policies that suits it? Public schools are also criticized for low achievement data, yet they are required by law to admit whoever comes through their doors. Meanwhile, private schools can establish whatever admission criteria they desire. Private schools have the resources to keep class sizes small, while public schools do not. This is the classic case of apples and oranges.

Or perhaps blueberries.

At a presentation to a group of teachers, during which he was blaming them for the sorry state of education, future education advocate and former ice cream company executive Jamie Vollmer was famously put in his place by a disgusted teacher who got him to admit that the quality of his company's famous blueberry ice cream was maintained by its firm stance on rejecting any substandard berries it received from its suppliers.[1]

Vollmer finally understood why public schools can't be run like businesses. And we should understand that, for the same reason, they can't be run like private schools either. But even if there actually were things a public school could be forced to learn from private schools, the idea of vouchers would still be unacceptable.

First, taking students out of a public school does not lower the cost of operating that school. As I'm sure you know, public education is funded by tax dollars. The percentage of those dollars a school receives is determined by the number of students it enrolls, so every student on the roster represents a piece of the pie. If the government issues a voucher to a student so they can attend a private school, that voucher is funded by "all or some of what the state would have otherwise spent to educate the child in a public school."[2] In short, your tax dollars will go toward your child's education if you use a government-issued voucher to send them to a private school, but you'll be skimming from the resources of your local public school if you do so.

Second, providing funding for voucher students to select private schools with religious affiliations violates the separation of church and state. This is not a debatable point.

Third, what does it say that our government supports the idea that students might find more success in schools run by teachers and administrators without the credentials it deems necessary for those it hires in its own schools—not to mention in schools free from the laws it puts in place to protect its students from discrimination?

Please also note that vouchers do not cover the full cost of tuition for most private schools, nor do they provide for transportation.

Which means they don't actually help the poor students for whom they were supposedly created.

Finally, and perhaps most importantly if you just don't care about the logic of these arguments because whatever it takes to get a student out of a bad school environment and into a good one works for you (an understandable position, frankly), evidence now abounds that none of the claims made by voucher advocates about how they'd improve our schools have actually come to pass.[3] As *The New York Times* reported in early 2017, "[A] wave of new research has emerged suggesting that private school vouchers may harm students who receive them. The results are startling—the worst in the history of the field . . ."[4]

Solution

One controversial solution (though less controversial than vouchers) are charters, which are government-authorized schools run by private organizations. Once approved and funded, they are permitted to operate with more freedom than traditional public schools.

It's true that students leaving for charter schools drain funds from the rest of the system just as damagingly as voucher students do. Even so, I would argue that within reason and if someone has a truly innovative plan, charter school experiments are worth the investment.

In theory.

Unfortunately, in reality, many charters operate with the freedom to do far more than innovate. As the Network for Public Education points out, "The public cannot review income and expenditures in detail. Many are for-profit entities or nonprofits that farm out management to for-profit corporations that operate behind a wall of secrecy."[5]

The result is that charter schools, as described recently by *Esquire* magazine, often become "vehicles for fraud and corruption."[6]

Furthermore, the twenty-five-year history of charter schools shows that they all too often fail to deliver on their promise of superior performance. According to the Center for Research on Educational Outcomes at Stanford, 75 percent of charter schools perform only as well as or worse than their local markets in reading and 71 percent in math.[7]

All that said, charter schools *can* become incubators for cutting-edge education, but they must be 100 percent as transparent as traditional public schools and held every bit as accountable. They should be approved with the utmost caution, and school districts must not hesitate to close those that do not get results. And charters should not be given a level of operational freedom impossible to transfer to traditional public schools—because that makes them nothing more than taxpayer-funded private schools.

Fortunately, some school districts are onto a better solution. They are opening a diverse array of "Option" (or Choice or Signature) schools, schools with distinctly different foci, from Drama to Computer Science to Culinary Arts. This diversity should extend to many other areas as well. Districts everywhere should be experimenting with nontraditional grading systems, flipped classrooms, multi-age classrooms, optional single-gender classrooms, and on and on—not in search of the "best" system, but to provide options for very different learners. If parents could select genuinely public school programs that suit their children's interests and needs, we'd finally have meaningful school choice.

Notes

1   Jamie Vollmer, "The Blueberry Story: The Teacher Gives the Businessman a Lesson," www.jamievollmer.com/blueberries.html.

2   Cory Turner, "School Vouchers 101: What They Are, How They Work—And Do They Work?" National Public Radio, December 7, 2016, https://www.npr.org/sections/ed/2016/12/07/504451460/school-choice-101-what-it-is-how-it-works-and-does-it-work.

3   Michael Pons, "School Vouchers: The Emerging Track Record," Nation Education Association, April 2002, www.nea.org/home/16970.htm.

4   Kevin Carey, "Dismal Voucher Results Surprise Researchers as DeVos Era Begins," *The New York Times*, February 23, 2017, accessed February 23, 2017, https://www.nytimes.com/2017/02/23/upshot/dismal-results-from-vouchers-surprise-researchers-as-devos-era-begins.html

5   Carol Burris, "The Network for Public Education Issues Its Position Statement on Charter Schools," Network For Public Education, May 31, 2017, accessed June 3, 2017, https://networkforpubliceducation.org/2017/05/network-public-education-issues-position-statement-charter-schools/.

6   Charles P. Pierce, "The Charter School Movement Is a Vehicle for Fraud and Corruption," *Esquire,* September 12, 2016, www.esquire.com/news-politics/politics/news/a48531/california-charter-schools/.

7   "National Charter School Study 2013," Center for Research on Education Outcomes January 2002, doi:10.4324/9781410605047.

Postscript

I would be remiss and, worse, totally unjust not to acknowledge in these pages that the American public school system is a truly heroic institution. To attempt to educate millions of children—*all* children—regardless of their gender, race, ethnicity, religion, sexual orientation, socioeconomic status, or disabilities is staggeringly ambitious. It is to our credit that we take for granted that such a thing is even possible. Given all the factors working against teachers, what they accomplish in this endeavor is nothing short of amazing.

That said, there are so many deeply embedded problems in our system that at times it feels beyond saving. Those included in this brief book are only the ones I feel able to address. There are, of course, many more. (Someone has to ease the burden on our poor, overworked Special Education teachers!) But the sheer volume of these issues can orient us in the right direction by putting the lie, once and for all, to the foolish notion that there is any sound-bite worthy answer to "what's wrong" with our schools.

Once we accept that our many challenges will require many solutions, we can roll up our sleeves and get down to the business of tackling them. Some, in fact, can be met easily. For example, there is no reason we must continue our obsession with standardized testing. Others, like rethinking the structure of the entire illogical system, will require some very heavy lifting.

Though it may seem otherwise, given this laundry list of complaints, I love being a teacher. That is because I have had the good fortune my entire career of being treated like a professional. That means I've been given creative leeway to accomplish my employers' goals the way I think best.

If absolutely nothing else changes, making sure all educators are treated as professionals would be transformative. Because in the end, it's not the latest teaching strategy, the "highest-yield" curriculum, the fanciest new "data harvesting" technique, or the most cutting-edge culture-building program that ultimately makes the difference—it is, and always has been, the *teacher*.

About the Author

David Michael Slater is a veteran middle and high school teacher who was named the City of Beaverton, Oregon's Educator of the Year in 2012. He is also an acclaimed author of over twenty works of fiction for children, teens, and adults. His work for children includes the picture books *Cheese Louise!*, *The Boy & the Book*, and *Hanukkah Harvie vs. Santa Claus*; the early chapter book series *Mysterious Monsters*; and the teen series *Forbidden Books*. David's work for adults includes the comic-drama *Fun & Games*, which the *New York Journal of Books* called "hilarious." David teaches in Reno, Nevada, where he lives with his wife and son. You can learn more about David and his work at www.davidmichaelslater.com.

Index

More Praise for *We're Doing It Wrong*

"Slater's initial four ideas encapsulate many of the changes in our society that have interfered with the delivery of a quality education in our public and private schools. We must take note of the 25 issues that he highlights as we move forward in addressing the future of our schools and the education of our children and youth in the 21st century."

—Paul A. Flexner
Instructor in Educational Psychology, Georgia State University
Co-editor of *What We NOW Know About Jewish Education*, winner of the
National Jewish Book Award

"This book opens the door to important conversations about education and how we can improve learning for all students."

—Catlin Tucker
Teacher, international trainer, speaker, and bestselling author

"David Michael Slater's *We're Doing It Wrong* calls a spade a spade. It is refreshing when educators offer ideas for change rather than simply deriding the status quo. While not all answers may work in every context, readers will discover some that could work anywhere."

—Dr. Carrie Geiger
University of Florida College of Education
P. K. Yonge Developmental Research School

"This book is timely in the world of education today. As an administrator in an elementary building, I know how critical it is to have teachers that are effective. I have said for many years that teachers are the most important factor in student success."

—Melissa Herek
2016 Wisconsin Elementary Principal of the Year

"This is a must-read for everyone from educators, to parents, to politicians. To use Slater's words, the solution to our problems lies not within a strategy or technique, 'it is, and always has been, the teacher.'"

—Courtney L. Cochran
2017 Arkansas Teacher of the Year

"The well-intentioned but misguided Educational Reform movement with its attempt to reduce student learning to data would do well to read David Michael Slater's book, *We're Doing It Wrong*. His focus on solutions makes his book a must-read for teachers and reformers alike. The fact is that teachers are the most effective reformers, and he wants the way cleared for them to be the best that they can be."

—Frank T. Lyman, Jr., PhD
Coauthor of *The Shaping of Thought* and author of *ThinkTrix*
Inventor and codeveloper of the Think Pair Share and ThinkTrix strategies

"In a period in which far too many books about what education policy should look like are written by 'experts' with no actual expertise in schools, David Michael Slater's *We're Doing It Wrong* provides a refreshing and much-needed dose of common sense. My biggest regret, after reading it, is that he didn't write this book earlier and that it thus didn't have the chance to influence policymaking over the past decade."

—Elaine Weise
National Coordinator for the Broader Bolder Approach to Education

"This is a vital book for anyone interested in improving education—policymakers, politicians, business people, educators, parents or students."

—Franklin Schargel
Author, consultant, former classroom teacher, school counselor,
school administrator
Winner of the 2016 "Hero Award" from Auburn University

"Slater's *We're Doing It Wrong* is a refreshingly honest and to-the-point review from a teacher's perspective—an important voice often drowned out by the drone of the experts and policymakers. Slater offers a wake-up call and reminder that while school systems continue to take one step forward and two steps back on the road to reform, children, especially our most vulnerable ones, pay the price."

—S. Kwesi Rollins, MSW
Director of Leadership Programs, Institute for Educational Leadership

"If you are passionate about the future of education, *We're Doing It Wrong* is a must-read! This book of hot-button issues and solutions should be read by school board members, parents, principals, and government officials in order to immediately begin radical change."

—Sarah L. Breckley
2017 Wisconsin High School Teacher of the Year
IIE AIFS Foundation Generation Study Abroad Fellow

"In his new book, David Michael Slater tells it as he sees it—from the front line as a middle school teacher. As a society, we could do much worse than to pay attention to Mr. Slater's warnings. This is required reading from a thoughtful, truthful, and articulate teacher."

—Faith Boninger,
National education policy expert

"In the spirit of Sir Ken Robinson, David Michael Slater explores how the current education system weeds out our most creative educators and leaves students unable to reach their full imaginative and innovative potential. Slater makes the case for creativity, and we couldn't agree more."

—Beth Miller
Executive Director, Creative Education Foundation

"In *We're Doing It Wrong*, David Michael Slater distills some of the most pressing issues in education into easy-to-read commonsense arguments. This is a must-read for anyone who is interested in exploring the quandary that education has found its way into and what hope we, as citizens, may have in helping to get it out.

—Eric Shyman
Author of *Vicious Circles in Education Reform* and
Reclaiming Our Children, Reclaiming Our Schools

"An innovative and necessary book, which I believe will speak to many teachers."

—Dr. Antonia Darder
Leavey Presidential Endowed Chair in Ethics and Moral Leadership,
School of Education, Loyola Marymount University, Los Angeles